NIMBUS

Glimpses of Vegetable Science

The Author

Dr. Udit Kumar, working as a capacity of Assistant Professor (SS), Department of Horticulture, Faculty of Agriculture, Dr. Rajendra Prasad Central Agricultural University, Pusa, Bihar and honored his Ph.D. degree in Horticulture (Vegetable Science) from G.B. Pant University of Agriculture and Technology, Pantnagar (Uttarakhand). He has also completed PG Diploma in Agriculture Extension Management from MANAGE, Hyderabad. He has also served as Subject Matter Specialist (Horticulture) at Krishi Vigyan Kendra of Birsa Agricultural University, Ranchi (Jharkhand).

He has thirty one full length research papers in national, international and foreign reputed Journals, 21 abstract, 21 book chapters and 29 Hindi and 7 English popular articles and 2 extension bulletins/book to his credit. He has also edited one books related to the field of Horticulture. Dr Kumar is the recipient of prestigious awards namely 'Excellence in teaching Award' in the year 2014 by the Society for Recent Development in Agriculture, Meerut(UP) and 'Young Scientist Award' for the year 2015 conferred by the G.K.V. Society, Agra(UP).

He is founder member of the Bihar Horticulture Society, Pusa, Bihar credited to him and was honoured for his outstanding contributions in strengthening the cause of the society. He is life member of nine national and international professional bodies and societies. Dr Kumar was also recognized by many national and international prestigious societies and exist as member of editorial board of Journal of Hill Agriculture and The Asian Journal of Horticulture, published by Indian Society of Hill Agriculture and Hind Agri-Hoticultural Society respectively. He has over twelve years experience as Teaching, Research and Extension in the field of Horticulture and handled projects as Principal Investigator like AICRP on Vegetable Crops, AINRP on Onion and Garlic, NHM (Vegetable Seed Production Programme), *etc*. More than 12 courses have been taught by him at Under Graduate and Post Graduate level.

NIMBUS

Glimpses of Vegetable Science

– Author –

Dr. Udit Kumar

Assistant Professor (SS)
Department of Horticulture, Faculty of Agriculture,
Dr. Rajendra Prasad Central Agricultural University,
Pusa, Bihar

BIOTECH

2021

BIOTECH BOOKS®

ISBN 978-81-7622-477-2

Published by: **BIOTECH BOOKS®**
4762-63/23, Ansari Road, Darya Ganj,
New Delhi - 110 002
Phone: 09899295259, 011-43003222
E-mail: biotechbooks@yahoo.co.in
Website: www.biotechbooks.in

Typeset at: **Classic Computer Services**
Delhi - 110 035

Printed at: ***Replika Press Pvt. Ltd.***

PRINTED IN INDIA

Preface

In the recent, the growing importance of vegetables has been recognized worldwide because of their vital role in food and nutrition security and their vital role in food and nutrition security and their emerging awareness on combing non-communicable diseases and health improvement.

The present book "**NIMBUS Glimpses of Vegetable Sciences**" is a compilation of latest information which provides an overview of concise and point wise information on vegetable crops. This book covers all vegetable sciences related area which includes vegetable production, vegetable breeding and postharvest technology. Most of the information is presented in tabular form in a comprehensive and lucid manner for easy understanding of the subject. Multiple choice questions fill in the blanks and true or false type of questions embedded in chapter will enable the readers to update their knowledge quickly and understanding of the subject in depth. This book is designed to serve as a handy guide for students, teachers, researchers and amateurs engaged in vegetable science. This book will also serves as a guide to the students to test their knowledge in the field of vegetable science as a whole. Special emphasis has been given to students appearing for various competitive examinations like post-graduate entrance examinations, SAUs Entrance, Ph.D., Junior Research Fellowship (JRF), Senior Research Fellowship (SRF), Agricultural Research Service (ARS), ICAR-National

Eligibility Test (NET), SET, Civil Services, Agricultural Officers, Bank P.O. (Agriculture), ADO and Allied Agricultural Examinations conducted by different agencies.

Dr. Udit Kumar

Contents

Chapter 1

Current Statistical Data of Vegetables

Statistical Datas of Vegetable Crops by NBH, Gurgaon (2018-19)

Total Horticulure (Indian Scenario)

- ☆ Area – 25.89 MHA, Production – 314.67 MT and Productivity – 11.84 MT/HA

Vegetable

- ☆ Area – 10.43 MHA
- ☆ Production – 187.97 MT
- ☆ Productivity – 17.3 MT/HA
- ☆ Growth rate of vegetables production during 2018-19 was **3.5 per cent** and area – 1.8 per cent
- ☆ Among horticulture vegetable production shares – 62.47 per cent

Crop-wise maximum area, production and productivity (2017-18)

Top 3 Area, Production and Productivity of Vegetables

	Area (Mha)	Rank	Production (MT)	Rank	Pdy (MT/HA)	Rank
Potato	2.18	1st	52.58	1st	21.5	3rd
Tomato	1.285	2nd	23.26	2nd	24.4	1st
Onion	1.29	3rd	23.67	3rd	21.2	7th
Tapioca	0.17	-	5.56	-	35.7	4th
Cabbage	0.40	-	9.91	-	22.6	2nd

Share of Vegetables Area and Production for State-Wise (2017-18)

State	*Area*	*Rank*	*Production*	*Rank*	*Pdy*	*Rank*
U.P	14.57	1st	28.32	1st		-
W.B.	14.00	2nd	27.69	2nd	21.3	3rd
M.P.	8.89	3rd	17.54	3rd		-
Bihar	8.24	4th	15.86	4th		
Pdy	-	-	-	-	35.3	1st (UT)
TN	-	-	-	-	29.9	1st
KL	-	-	-	-	22.7	2nd
J and K	-	-	-	-	22.4	4th

W.B – West Bengal, UP – Uttar Pradesh, Pdy – Pondicherry, TN – Tamilnadu, KL – Kerala, J and K – Jammu and Kashmir and UT – Union Territory.

Global Vegetable Scenario

- ☆ Area – 53.97 MHA, Production – 1012.52 MT and Productivity – 18.8MT/HA
- ☆ India 1st in Production of okra –73 per cent
- ☆ India 2nd in Production (After China) – Brinjal, Cabbage, Cauliflower, Onion, Potato and Tomato

Major Vegetable Producing Country in World (2010-11)

Country	*Area (MHA)*	*Production (MHA)*	*Per cent Share*	*Pdy (MT/HA)*
China	21.047	473.06	48	-
India	8.495	146.55	14	-
USA	1.123	35.293	3	31.4 (2nd)

Country	*Area (MHA)*	*Production (MHA)*	*Per cent Share*	*Pdy (MT/HA)*
Turkey	1.089	-	3	-
Spain	-	-	-	37.2 (1st)
Iran	-	-	-	26.2 (3rd)

Chapter 2

Current Directors of Vegetable Science Network

Year 2017-18

- Secretary and Director General of ICAR

  Dr. Trilochan Mohapatra

- ICAR–CPRI – Central Potato Research Institute, Kufri, Shimla, Himachal Pradesh

  Director – Shri N. Murugesan

  Sub-Stations – Kufri, Modipuram, Patna, Jalandhar, Gwalior, Shillong, Ooty

- ICAR– IIHR – Indian Institute of Horticulture, Hessaraghatta, lake post, Bengaluru

  Director – Dr. A.S. Sidhu

- ICAR–IIHR Head – **Dr. A.T. Sadashiva**, Principal Scientist and Head, Division of Vegetable Crops, Specialisation: Vegetable Breeding (Solanaceous Crops)

- ICAR–CISH – Central Institute for Subtropical Horticulture, Rehmankehra, Lucknow

  Director – Dr. Shailendra Rajan

- ICAR–CIAH – Central Institute of Arid Horticulture, Beechwal, Bikaner, Rajasthan

  Director – Dr. B.D. Sharma

- ICAR–NRC for seed spices, Ajmer, Rajasthan

  Director – Dr. Balraj Singh

- ICAR–IIVR – Indian Institute of Vegetable Research, Jakhini (Shahanshahpur), Varanasi – Uttar Pradesh

  Project Co-ordinator, for AICRP on Vegetable Crops **Dr. B. Singh**

  Director – Dr. Jagdish Singh

- **Dr Anand Kumar Singh,** Deputy Director General (Horticultural Science) Division of Horticulture, Krishi Anusandhan Bhawan - II, New Delhi

- **Dr. A.K. Singh**, Deputy Director General (Agricultural Extension) Division of Agricultural Extension, Krishi Anusandhan Bhawan, New Delhi

- **Dr. Trilochan Mohapatra**, Secretary (DARE) and Director General (ICAR) Krishi Bhavan, New Delhi.

- ICAR–CTCRI - Central Tuber Crops Research Institute, Thiruvananthapuram, Kerala.

  Director – Dr. Archana Mukherjee

Chapter 3

General Vegetable Science

Father of Vegetable Science – **L.H. Bailey**

Parthenocarpy

- ☆ Parthenocarpy term coined by Null (1902)
- ☆ Parthenocarpy in vegetable cucumber, watermelon and tomato by single recessive gene (pat-2)
- ☆ Artificial parthenocarpy induced by tomato(IAA, GA3) and brinjal (2,4-D and IAA)

Boidiversity

- ☆ PPV and FRA act, 2001 and Rules, 2003
- ☆ PPV and FRA located at New Delhi
- ☆ Biodiversity international is located at, Rome, Italy, 1974
- ☆ National biodiversity authority (NBA), Taramani, Chennai, Tamil Nadu
- ☆ Indian patent Act, 2005
- ☆ Invention on biological diversity, 1992
- ☆ Biological diversity Act, 2002 and Rules, 2003

Hydroponics

- ☆ Father of hydroponics **Dr. William F Gericke**, USA

- In India first introduced at Kalimpong, Darjeeling district, WB
- Optimum pH of solution: **5.2-6.5**
- Max area under cultivation : Israel
- First crop raised in the hydroponics : Tomato cv. Pipo
- Soilless culture technique : Nutrient film technique (NFT) and Aeroponics

Organic Farming

- Area – 4.48 MH and India maximum area in MP
- Sikkim is a organic state in India ≈ 75,000 ha of agricultual land.
- Austria (Mendal origin) is Maximum Producer in Globe
- **NPOP** – National Programme on Organic Production, Launched at 2001 under FTDR Act (Foreign Trade Development and Regulation Act)
- **NCOF** – National Centre for Organic Farming at Ghaziabad, UP
- **NPOF** – National Project on Organic Farming at 2004
- **IFOAM** – International Federation of Organic Agriculture Movements (1972) at Germany

Chapter 4

Vegetable Research Achievements

Vegetable Research Achievement in India Since Past 40 Years

- 1916 – First hybrid research in world Hays and Jones 1933 – Hybrid vigour in chilli
- 1935, 1940 – popular F1 hybrid developed cucumber and tomato
- 1940 – Research started for tem. Vegetables at Quetta (Now in Pakistan) 1947 – Nucleus plant introduction scheme at IARI by Dr. Harbajan Singh 1948 – CPRI started at shimla, HP
- 1949 – Vegetable breeding station starting at Katrain, Kullu Valley, HP 1956 – Division of horticulture started (Before Division of Botany) at IARI
- 1968 – IIHR, Hessaraghatta, Bengaluru improvement of Tropical Vegetable
- 1970-71 – AICVIP was started during 4th FYP (1st coordinator Dr. Vishnu swarup) 1973 – 1st hybrid released Tomato(Karnataka) and Capsicum(Bharat) by IAHS 1973 – Fist public sector F1 hybrid in : Bottle gourd (Pusa Meghdoot)
- 1986 – started for PDVR at IARI, New Delhi 1991 – Dr. Kalloo joining 1st PDVR

- ☆ 1992 – Shifting the head Quarter PDVR; IARI, Delhi to Varanasi, UP 1994 – NRC for Onion and Garlic, Pune
- ☆ 1999 – Upgradation of PDVR to IIVR
- ☆ 2009 – NRC for Onion and Garlic changed to Directorate of Onion and Garlic

Chapter 5

Vegetable Cultivation Points to Ponder

1) Tomato

- ☆ Father of tomato breeder : Dr. C.M. Rick, California USA
- ☆ Tomato genetic cooperative is located at university of California, USA
- ☆ Tomato fruit contain aroma due to sulfonium
- ☆ pH for processing tomato is <4.5
- ☆ Tomato ripening mutants for increase shelf life are **rin, nor** and **nr**
- ☆ Seed yiedls of tomato are 100-120kg/ha
  - ❒ Best method of tomato seed extraction is Alkali method – 10 per cent washing soda
  - ❒ Beta carotene rich varieties are Caro – Rich and Caro – Red
- ☆ Tomato variety suitable for processing are Pusa Sheetal, Roma, Pant Bahar and Pusa Saurabh.
- ☆ Indeterminate variety are Sioux, Marglobe, Best of all(USA) and Pusa Ruby
- ☆ Determinate variety are Roma, Pusa Chhuhara and Pusa Sheetal
- ☆ Most severe disease of tomato are TLCV mainly in autumn winter in NI planis transmitted by whitefly yield loss around 90 per cent

2) Brinjal

- Brinjal discoloration is due to polyphenol oxidase enzyme
- Glucoalkaloid solasodine is responsible for bitter tast in brinjal
- Favourable temperature for brinjal production 21-27°C
- Fruit setting range from long style 70-86 per cent, medium style 12.55- 55.6 per cent and no in short style
- Application of 2,4-D @ 2ppm induce parthenocarpy fruit set and increase yield

3) Chilli

- Green chilli rich in rtin (Vit – P) against cancer
- India major producer, consumer and exporter (AP – leading producer June to Oct)
- Capsaicin mostly 90 per cent present in placenta of chilly fruits
- Chemical formula for capsanthin $C_{40}H_{56}O_3$ and capsaicin $C_{18}H_{27}NO_3$
- Yellow colour sp. of chilly *C. baccatum*
- Purple color flowering chilly *C. pubescens, C. eximium* and *C. Cardensii*
- Powdery mildew resistant chilly ssp *C. pubescens* and *C. Baccatum*
- Heatness of chilli measured by Scoville Heat Units (SHU)

4) Okra

- Okra warm season crop rich in iodine
- Okra genus Abelmoschus was firast established by Medikus in 1987
- Cultivated ssp of okra are *A.esculenta, A. manihot* and *A. moschata*
- Scientist Dr. Harbhajan Singh started systematic research work in India
- Okra sp. resistant to low temp. *Abelmoschus angulosus*
- Resistant to YVMV *A. pungens* (**), *A. tuberculatus* – progenitor of cultivated okra (symptomless resistant), *A. manihot* (Ghana okra) and *A.m* ssp. *manihot* (highest chr. No 2n=194)
- Seed rate for summer crop 18-20kg/ha and RF 10-12kg/ha.

- ✰ Temperature for seed germination <20°C no germination, germination at 25-35°C and at 35°C faster germination observed

Major Problem in Seed Production is Seed Shattering

- ✰ Parentage of Punjab – 7, Punjab Padmini and Parbhani Kranti (*A. esculentus x A. manihot ssp. manihot*)
- ✰ Parentage of Arka Abhay and Arka Anamika are (*A. esculentus x A. tetraphyllus*)

Importance of Brassica Vegetable Crops

- ✰ Among cruciferus vegetable high Vit – A: Kale followed by broccoli
- ✰ Among cruciferus crops maximum Vit – C: Kale followed by Brussels sprout
- ✰ Cross pollination is due to self-incompatability and protogyny
- ✰ Among cole crops max. Cross pollination broccoli 95 per cent and lowest Brussels sprout 72 per cent
- ✰ Interspecific hybrids of cole crops Hakuran (cabbage x Chinese cabbage) Rutabaga/swede (turnip x cabbage) and *Rapano brassica* (radish x cabbage)
- ✰ The book cole crop written by Nieuwhof
- ✰ Brassica U triangle gave by Nagaharu (1935)
- ✰ Maturity of cabbage or head compactness determined by Pearson formula, $Z = (C \times 100)/W^3$
- ✰ Maturity of cabbage 1st round type followed by conical(jersey wakefield)
- ✰ Cabbage yellow is caused by *F oxy f. Conglutinans*
- ✰ Black leg more commen in saline soil (*Phoma lingam*)
- ✰ Cauliflower was introduced to India in 1822 by Dr. Jemson from England
- ✰ Among cole crop cauliflower only racememose others cyme
- ✰ Scooping operation in cauliflower for initiation of flower stalk
- ✰ F1 hybrid of cauliflower are Pusa Hybrid-2, Pusa Karthik Sankar and Arka Kanti

- Self blanched var of cauliflower Pusa Deepali, Pusa Himjyoti and all late variety
- Cauliflower var. Resistant to curd and inflorescence blight – Pusa Snowball K-1
- Blotch rot resistant varieties Pusa Katki, Pusa Shubhra and Pusa Snowball K-1
- Knol khol is most popular in kashmir 800-1000g/ha high seed rate among cole crops)
- Important var. of knol khol are White Vienna, Purple Vienna, King of North, **Palam Tenderknob** and **Pusa Virat**
- Highest area for broccoli at HP, rich source of sulphoraphane
- Optimum temperature for proper head formation is 12-18°C.
- New Broccoli variety Palam Kanchan – yellowish green (head type), Palam Vichitra – purple (head type), Palam Haritika and Palam Samridhi (green color – sprouting type)

Cucurbitaceae Vegetables

- The word Cucurbit coined by Dr.L.H. Bailey
- Among cucurbits bitter gourd rich in Vit – C, pumpkin rich in carotene (Vit-A)
- Bitter principles of cucurbits due to presence of cucurbitacins (tetracycline triterpenes)
- Cucurbit sex ratio range are 15:1 or 25-30:1
- Primitive sex form of cucurbits hermaphrodite
- First Gynocious F1 hybrid developed in India is Pusa Sanyog in 197 scientist De candolle (1967) cucumber indigenous to India
- Horticultural classification of muskmelon gave by Naudin (1859) and modified by Munger and Robinson (1991)
- Snapmelon *C.m.var. momordica* resistant to PM, DM and CGMMV
- Resistant to fruit fly ssp in muskmelon *Cucumis callosus*
- Resistant to nematode are C *anguria,* C *ficifolia* and C *metuliferus*
- Seedless watermelon variety Arka Madhura (suitable for round year in GH) and Pusa Bedana

- ✰ Bitter gourd are cross incompatible with *M. dioica x M. balsamina*
- ✰ Dioeious sp. of bitter gourd spine gourd/kartoli *M. cochinchinensis* (rich beta carotene), teasle gourd: *M. subangolata* ssp. *Renigera*
- ✰ Snake gourd flower color – white (bottle gourd and Ivy gourd also white flower)
- ✰ Bottle gourd Pusa Meghdoot (PSPL x sel. 2) and Pusa Manjari (PSPL x Sel.11)
- ✰ Popular Ayurvedic **Kooshmanda Rasayam** prepared from Ashgourd
- ✰ Anthesis time of Ridge gourd evening (4-7pm) and sponge gourd morning time (6- 8am) so these two sp. cross in-compatible
- ✰ Chowchow are viviparous germination habit (>3 or 4 sprouts)

Peas and Beans

Peas are good source of digestible protein (7 per cent)

- ✰ Ancestor of pea *Pisum elatius*
- ✰ Horticultural pea: *Pisum sativum* var. *hortense,* edible podded pea *P s var. macrocarpum*
- ✰ Dwarf pea : *P. Humile*
- ✰ UP is leading peas growing state in India
- ✰ Shelling per cent of pea 35-45 per cent
- ✰ Protein content of wrinkled peas is more (33 per cent) compare to smooth seeded pea (23- 31 per cent)
- ✰ Round seeded variety tolerant to high temperature compared to smooth one
- ✰ **S. Blixt** famous garden pea breeder or father of pea breeding in World
- ✰ Optimum temp. for pea seed germination 22°C
- ✰ Seed rate of early pea 100-120kg/ha and mid and late 80-90kg/ha
- ✰ Sowing time of pea in NI plains October–mid November.
- ✰ Tendrometer (Heat unit – 4.4°C) is a machine used to determine maturity

- **Leafless pea** – *Afila* tolerant to water-logging, non-lodging, resistant to disease and suitable for mechanical harvest
- Resistant to powdery mildew (single ressive gene er-1 and er-2) in Pea var. Pusa Pragati, Arka Karthik, Arka Sampoorna, Palam Priya and Arka Ajit
- Edible podded pea UN-53, Sylvia, Arka Sampoorna and Mithi Phali
- Wrinkled seeded peas used for dehydration (Arkel and Bonneville)
- Progenitor of French bean *Phaseolus aborigineus*
- Drought tolerant *P. acutifolius* and salinity tolerant *P. filiformios*
- Seed rate for bush French bean 65kg/ha and pole type 25-30kg/ha
- Hypocotyl cracking or necrosis in French bran due to low Ca content in seed
- Photo insensitive French bean cultivars are Arka Suvidha, Arka Komal, Arka Anoop, Arka Sharath and Arka Bold
- Exotic introduced var. of French bean Contender (USA), Bountiful (USA), Jampa (Mexico), Giant Stringless and Premier (Sweden)
- Introduced variety of Indian bean are Dasarawal, Deepaliwal and Rajini
- New var of Indian bean Arka Sambhram, Arka Soumya and Arka Bold (mutany variety)
- Golden mosaic virus in in Indian bean caused by white fly
- Guar gum extracted from cluster bean seed it contain 68-70 per cent galactomannan
- Goma Manjari cluster bean var. resistant to PM, leaf spot and bacterial blight
- Ancestral cowpea are *Vigna unguiculata* var. *mensensii*
- Photoinsensitive cow pea var. Arka Garima, Arka Suman, Arka Samrudhi and Arka Mangala
- Resistant to golden mosaic virus and photoinsensitive are Kashi Sudha, K Kanchan, K Unnati and K Gauri
- Winged bean is 20th century vegetable, whole plant are edible and also called as god sent vegetable

Bulb Vegetables

- ☆ Onion is cool season and shallow rooted vegetable
- ☆ Yellow colour of onion (outer) skin is due to Quercetin
- ☆ Enzyme contain in onion is allinase
- ☆ India is 3rd major exporter after Netherland (21 per cent) and Spain
- ☆ India major producer MH and high paddy in Gujarat (32t/ha)
- ☆ NHRDF, Nasik, MH and Directorate of Onion and Garlic 2009 (After change NRC for O and G)
- ☆ Ancestor of onion *Allium vavilovi* SN of tree onion (*A c* var *aggregatum*), leek (*A c* var *porrum*) and Kurrat (*A. kurrat*)
- ☆ Allium royalei ssp resistant to downey mildew, leaf blight and used for bridging ssp
- ☆ Bulb color of onion is controlled by 5 major gene (ICGLR) and bulb shape by multiple gene
- ☆ Optimum tem. for seed germination (20-25°C), Vegetative growth (13-23°C) and bulb (15-21°C)
- ☆ Onion cross pollination is due to protandey
- ☆ Flower colour – white or blue
- ☆ Onion CGMS reported S and T cytoplasm but S type mostly used for hybrid seed production
- ☆ Dr. H.A. Jones from University of California 1st identified CMS in Italian red lines
- ☆ Seed rate for kharif 12-15kg/ha and rabi 10-12kg/ha and bulb requirement 1000-1200 kg/ha
- ☆ Herbicide used to control weeds in Onion Pendimethalin 3.5l/ha or Oxyfurofan 0.25kg/ha
- ☆ Ideal storage temperature for onion 0°C at 65-75 per cent RH
- ☆ Ideal TSS for dehydration >18 per cent and desired drying ratio 10:1
- ☆ Most destructive disease of onion are purple blotch (28-30°C and 80-90 per cent RH) and pest thrips
- ☆ Two hybrid (F1) of onion Arka Lalima and Arka Kirthiman by using CMS line

- Pusa Madhvi of onion developed through selfing and massing
- Brown Spanish onion var. suitable for long day cultivation
- Onion variety suitable for both Kharif and Rabi (Arka Pitambhar and Arka Niketan
- Onion variety suitable for kharif cultivation N-53, Arka Kalian, Agrifound dark red, N- 2-4-1 and Baswant-180
- Leek is non bulb forming onion family and tetraploid ssp
- Exotic var. London flag and American flag and Palam Paushtic (indigenous in India)
- Amcestor of garlic *Allium longicupis*
- Non bolting garlic *A. sativum* var. *sativum* and *Bolting* ssp. (*A s* var. *Ophiosorodon)*
- Garlic sexually sterile diploid plant

Root Vegetables

- Bitter flavour Isocoumarine is responsible for bitter flavor in carrot
- Centre of origin of carrot is Afghanistan 9 from Queen anns lace *D. carota* ssp. *carota*
- Carrot red colour due to lycopene, orange colour dur to beta-carotene, purple colour due to anthocyanin and yellow colour due to Xanthophyll (lutein) carrot inflorescence is compound umbel and fruit type Schizocarp
- Carrot 3 type of male sterility 10 brown anther(available in tender sweet var.) and 20 petaloid anther(available in cornel wild) 30 Gummifer type
- Petaloid type commercially using but brown anther type commonly using in Korean country.
- Optimum temperature for seed germination 7-23°C and color development 15-21°C
- Carrot variety Chantenay suitable for excellent canning
- Pusa Nayanjyoti first temperate carrot hybrid developed by using CMS
- Pusa Vasuda first tropical carrot hybrid developed by using CMS

- New var. of carrot Pusa Asita (**Black**) and Pusa Rudhira (**Red**) and Pusa Payasa mustard color
- Tropical carrot Pusa Kesar, Pusa Meghali and Pusa Vasuda and temperate carrot Pusa Yamadangi
- Exotic poipular carrot var. Chantenay- abrupt blund tip variety, Zeno from Germany suitable for Nilgiris in Ooty, Danvers, Nantes and Early Horn and Early Gem
- Heat tolerant carrot: Kuroda and New Kuroda from Japan deep orange and stumped
  - Banga (1976) gave the botanical variety of different carrot (Eurpian, oil/Foder, Rat-tail, Spanish and Japanese radish)
- Glucose is major sugar present in radish and shape of radish is fusiform
- Radish pungency due to Isothiocyanates and it is most ancient among root crop
- Anthocyanin present in red, purple and pink color carrot
- Fruit is siliqua and inflorescence is terminal raceme temperature suitable for radish cultivation 10-15°C and best flavour, texture and size at 15-21°C
- First reported Ogura type male sterility in Japanese carrot by Ogura (1968)
- Seed rate for tropical carrot 8-10kg/ha and temperate carrot 10-12kg/ha
- The Japanese white can set the seed in North Indian plain condition
- New variety of radish are Palam Hriday, Pusa Jamuni, Pusa Gulabi and Pusa Mridula

Radish Variety

Rapid red white tipped, Scarlet Globe and French breakfast	Round or globular shape
Pusa Ahuka	Green shoulder varity
Pusa Sagarika	First purple radish variety
Pusa Vidhu	Long field staying capacity
Pusa Mridula	Suitable for kitchen garden

- Beet roor origin from sea beat *Beta vulgaris* ssp. *maritima*
- The cross between Beetroot x sugarbeet are cross compatible
- Red violet color carrot due to beta-cyanin pigment and yellow color due to beta- xanthin
- Beet root seed is seed ball or multigerm it contain 2-6 seeds
- Beet root seed production only in hill and dia m 3.5cm suitable for harvest
- Insect aphid in beet root responsible transmission of mosaic disease poor color development and dzoning of beet due to high warm weather temperature during root developemt
- Boron deficiency in beet commonly present in alkaline soil var Avon early resistant to bolting and DM
- Variety used for monogerm cultivation are Khavskaya
- Turnip is a modified form of tap root it is napiform shape
- Turnip classification gave by Shoemaker (1949)
- Seed rate 5-6kg/ha, turnip yellow mosaic virus transmitted by flea beetle
- Pusa Kanchan variety set seeds in plains of north India

Tuber Crops

- Potato is also called as poor man's friend/poor mans strength
- India is 3rd highest producer and 4th major area in globe
- Potato is self pollinated crop and potato rich in Vit-C
- Potato is auto-tetraploid 2n=48(x = 12) or segmented allopolyploid
- Potato tuber rich source of carbohydrate (CHO) contain 22.6 per cent and 60-80 per cent starch
- International year of potato was 2008 by United States
- Optimum temperature for periderm formation 15-20°C and optimum temperature for tuberization 18-20°C
- Potato sprouting temperature at 22-34°C
- Diploid ssp fo potato *S. phureja* and *S. stenotomum* pentaploid ssp *S. curtilobum* (2n=60)

- Highly resistant to late blight ssp *S. bulbocastanum* (**Hexaploid ssp**) and *S. demissum*
- Resistant to cyst nematode *S. vernei*
- Seed plot technique (SPS) developed by Pushkarnath (1967) by CPCRI for multiplication of seed tuber free from virus in NI plains and TPS concept gave by Dr. S. Ramanujam
- Seed rate for TPS 100-120g/ha and using tuber by 800-1500kg/ha
- Suberization temperature of potato is 25°C and 75-80 per cent RH
- **Breaking of potato dormancy** by soak the tuber *1 per cent thiourea + 1ppm GA3 @ 1 hour*
- Commonly used **sprout suppresent** is *CIPC or Chloropropham 25mg a.i/kg* of tubers
- Dehaulming (Removal of vegetative part) done before aphid reaching critical level 20 Aphid/100 leaves
- International potato centre (CIP) is located at Peru in 1971
- Major problem for potato cultivation in South Indian hill is golden cyst nematode
- Early potato variety (80-90days) Kufri Chandramukhi, K Jawakar, K Laukar, K Sheetman, K Khyati, K Ashoka and K Surya *(Heat tolerant variety)*
- **Kufri badshah is MDR** (Resistant to Late blight, Early blight and Potato virus X)

Potato Processing Variety

Variety	*Purpose*
Kufri Surya	Early maturity, heat tolerant, french fries and chips
Kufri Frysona	French fries
Kufri Chipsona-3	Resistant to late blight (medium)
Kufri Chipsona-4	Resistant to late blight (early)
Kufri Chipsona-1	Chips and French fries
Kufri Chipsona-2	Chips and flakes
Kufri Himsona	Chips and flakes

- ☆ Potato variety restant to frost: Kuri Sheetman and Kufri Chipsona-2
- ☆ Resistant to potato cyst nematode and late blight: Kufri Swarna and Kufri Thenamalai

Important Potato Disorder

Physiological Disorder	*Causes*
Internal bron spot	Moisture deficiency
Hollow heart	Excessive nitrogen
Black heart	Starvation of O_2 or Poor Ventilation in room

- ☆ Sweet potato is cheapest source of calories and hexaploid in nature
- ☆ Sweet potato generally growing in India rain fed crop and drought tolerant crop
- ☆ *Ipomia trifida* is progenitor of sweet potato
- ☆ Ideal temperature for cultivation >24°C and tuber formation 20-30°C
- ☆ Propagation through vine cutting 40,000-50,000 cutting/ha
- ☆ Sweet potato weevil most serious pest of sweet potato causes severe damage in summer season crop

Sweet Potato Variety

Variety	*Var./hybrid*	*Purpose*
Sree Bhadra	Clonal selection	Excellent trap crop for rootknot nematode
Sree Vardhini	Clonal selection	Purple skin and yellow flesh
Sree Rethna	Hybrid	Purple flesh and orange flesh
Sree Nandhini	Clonal selection	Suitable for drought tolerant
Sree Lanaka	Hybrid	Short duration, rich in beta-carotene variety and suitable for industrial purpose
Sree Varun	Hybrid	
Sree Arun	Hybrid	
Pusa Sunheri	-	Flesh light orange and rich in carotene, suitable for industrial purpose
Pusa Lal	-	Best shelf life
Pusa Bharati	-	Good Vit-C and beta-carotene
Pusa Safed	-	Excellent cooking quality

- ☆ Tapioca is a perennial, monoecious and drought tolerant crops
- ☆ Nigeria is leading country for Cassava production
- ☆ In India tapioca grown rainfed crop in Kerala and AP and irrigated crop in TN
- ☆ Cassava highest production and productivity in Tamil Nadu
- ☆ Yellow colour of cassava is due to presence of beta-carotene (precursor of Vit A)
- ☆ Cassava is highly cross pollinated and monoecious due to protoandry
- ☆ Cassava mosaic virus (CMV) is most serious disease transmitted by whitefly
- ☆ Cassava variety suitable for industrial purpose H-7, H-165, H-226(most preferred 28- 30 per cent starch)
- ☆ Tapioca hybrid suitable for stable purpose Sree Sahya (multiple hybrid starch 38-41 per cent) and Sree Visakam (rich in beta-carotene)
- ☆ Tapioca variety suitable for short duration Sree Jaya, Sree Pralash and Sree Vijaya
- ☆ Sree Rekha and Sree Prabha suitable for low and upland cultivation
- ☆ Sree Padmanabha var. of cassava resistant to cassava mosaic disease (CMD)
- ☆ Sree Harsha is triploid hybrid (starch 36-40 per cent) and Sree Sahaya (multiple hybrid)
- ☆ Non-branching variety of cassava are Nidhi, KMC-1 and M-4
- ☆ Ethylene chlorohydrine (4-8 per cent) is used for break the dormancy of yam
- ☆ Ideal tuber weight for planting of greater yam 200-250g and white yam 100-125g
- ☆ Among the yam ***white yam need of staking*** (support) to grow the wines
- ☆ Greater yam variety are Sree Keerthi, Sree Roopa, Sree Karthika and Sree Shilpa (1st hybrid)
- ☆ Lesser yam var. are Sree Latha and Sree Kala

- White yam variety Sree Subhra, Sree Priya and Sree Dhanya (dwarf var no need for staking)

Leafy Vegetables

- Amaranrhus is a bacially warm season, C4 plant and pollination through wind
- Fruit type of amaranth is glomerule and fruit is utricle
- Amaranth triploid ssp. *A. dubius*, day neutral *A. hypochandriacus*, short day ssp. *A. cruentus* and parental sp. are *A. caudatus*
- Seed rate of amaranthus for transplanting 1kg and direct method 2kg/ha
- Leaf and stem ratio of amaranthus is >1
- Badi chauli *A. tricolor* and Chhoti Chaulai *A. blitum*
- Pusa Lal Chauli stem deep red color suitable for dye extraction and ornamental purpose
- Malabar Spinach or Poi or Basella is rich in Vit-A
- Seed rate of basella 12-15kg/ha, red type (*B. rubra* 2n=44 and green *B. alba* 2n-48)
- Seed rate of palak or spinach beet 25-30kg/ha (summer crop) and winter(10-15kg/ha)
- Palak var. Jobner Green tolerant to high pH (10.5), Pusa Bharati high Vit-C and beta-carotene, Pusa Jyoti colchicines induced polyploidy (2 per cent) and all green
- Parentage of Pusa Harit (Sugar Beet x Local Palak), Pusa Palk (Swiss Chard x Local Palak) both are late bolting type
- Flower colour of common Methi white, quich growing and kasuri methi flower color bright orange and yellow, slow growing
- Pusa Early Bunching is a improved var. of fenugreek

Important Scientist and Contribution

Scientist	*Contribution*
Miller	Coined *Lycopersicon esculentum*
Muller (1940)	Classified genus *Lucopersicon* into sub genus
Hedric and Booth	1st tomato linkage map and heterosis

Scientist	*Contribution*
Kakizaki (1931)	1st reported heterosis in brinjal
Zeven and Zhukovsky (1975)	Okra Hindustan origin
Medicus (1787)	Established genus Abelmoschus
Dr. Harbhajan Singh	Systematic work in okra
Peterson and Weigle (1958)	Gynocious line in cucumber
Jeffrey (1983)	Cucumis classification
Chakravarty (1982)	Classification of cucurbitaceae 39genera and 825 ssp
WA orton (1911)	Fusarium wilt in watermelon
Naudin (1859)	Muskmelon classification
Bohn and Whittaker (1949)	Reported recessive MS line gene ms-1
T A More and Sheshadari (1980)	Developed tropical true gynocious line
Nagaharu (1935)	Developed brassica U triangle
Stout (1917)	Term self incompatability
Banga (1976)	Radish classification
Ogura (1968)	First reported CMS in radish
Munger (1953)	Petaloid cytoplasm in carrot (var Cornell)
Welch and Grimball (1947)	Brown anther(var. Tender sweet)
T. Nothangel (1992)	Gummefer MS(ssp D. Dummifer)
Jones and Emsweller	CGMS in Italian red var of onion
Jones and Dais (1944)	CGMS was 1st report inheritance in onion

Chapter 6

Plant Growth Regulators

Plant Growth Regulators in Vegetable Production

Crops	*Growth Regulators (ppm)*	*Functions*
Tomato	2,4-D @ 2-5	Parthenocarpy, Seed treatment
Brinjal	2,4-D @ 2	Improve fruit set
Chilli	GA_3 @ 10, NAA @ 40	Enhance fruit set
Watermelon	TIBA @ 25-50	Induction of more female flower
Cucunber	Ethereal @ 150-200	Increase female flower production
	$AgNO_3$ @ 200-300	Induction of male flower
Summer Squash	Ethephon @ 250	Suppression of male flower
	Ethephon @ 600	Complete suppression of male flower
Garden pea	CCC @ 50	Increase drought tolerance
	GA_3 @ 50	Increase the yield
Onion	MH @ 1500-2000	Sprout suppresent
Potato	Thiourea 1 per cent	Breaking the tuber dormancy
	CIPC 25mg/tonn tuber (Oorja solution form)	Used for Sprout inhibitors of storage potato
	MH	Sprout inhibitors
	GA3 @ 10-15	Breaking the tuber dormancy and Enhance the sprouting

Chapter 7

Biotechnology and Molecular Markers

- Father of tissue culture **Dr. Gottlieb Haberlandt (1964)**
- Embryo culture technology done more in *Brassica*
- Production of homozygous plant from double haploid and androgenisis commonly used technique for double haploid production
- Cybrid means (crossing of nuclear gene from one plant + cytoplasm from one plant)
- Term MAS first used by **Beckmann and Soller** (1986)
- Polymerase chain reaction (PCR) developed by **Dr. Karry Mullis** (1985)
- Hybridization based marker : RFLP
- PCR based marker SSR, RAPD and AFLP
- Dominant markers – RAPD, AFLP, ISSR and SCAR
- Co-dominant marker – RFLP, SSR, SNP, SRAP and STS
- Marker used for diversity analysis RAPD and ISSR
- SSR marker used for analysis of F_1 hybrid purity test and diversity analysis
- Mapping populations are F_2 generation, Back cross generations, RIL and DH

- ☆ QTL – Quantitative Traits Loci, term firast coined by Gelderman (1975)
- ☆ First tagged QTL plant fw 2.2 for fruit weight in tomato
- ☆ Leading transgenic plant producing countries are USA, Argentina and Canada

Genome Sequencing in Vegetable Crops

Crop	*Genome in Size (Mbp)*	*Lines*	*Year of Developed*
Cucumber	367	Chinese long - 9930	2009
Chinese cabbage	283.8	Chiifu – 401-42	2011
Potato	844	RH 89-039-16 and DM – 1-3-516R44	2011
Tomato	900	Heinz 1706	2012
Watermelon	375	DHL92	2012
S. pimpincllifolium	739	LAI589	2012
Melon	450	Double haploidline-DHL-92	2012

Transgenic Varieties in Vegetable Crops

Crop	*Purpose/Aim*	*Varieties*	*Year*	*Company*
Tomato	Improve shelf life	Flavr savr	1994	Calgene
	Improve shelf life	Endless summer	1995	DNA plant Technology
Potato	Bt gene (Resistant to colorado potato beetle)	New leaf	1995	Monsanto
	Resistant to virus	Freedom II	1995	Ashgrow seeds
	Bt gene and PLRV	New leaf plus	1998	Monsanto
	Resistant to Colorado beetle	Elizabeth	2010	Monsanto

Transgenic Developments in Vegetable Crops

Crops	*Genes*	*Scientist*	*Against/Resistant*
Potato	Bt Cry 1Ab		Potato tuber moth
Tomato	Cry 1Ab		Fruit borer
Brinjal	Cry 1Ab		Shoot and fruit borer
Cabbage	Cry 1Hc/Cry 9C		Lepidopteron insect
Cucumber and Watermelon	DefH9-iaaM		Parthenocarpy
Potato	AmA1	Datta (1997)	Protein rich potato

Crops	*Genes*	*Scientist*	*Against/Resistant*
Golden Potato	Crtb, Crti and Crty from Erwinia	Diretto (2007)	Pro-vitamin Acarotenoids
Brinjal and Tomato	Chitinase, glucanase and thaumatin		Fungal
Tomato	CHI from Petunia hybrida	Verhoeyen (2002)	Improving antioxidant level
Cassava	Asp1	Zhang (2003)	Improvement of protein content
Sweet potato	Asp1	Prakash (1997)	Improvement of protein content
Lettuce	Ferritin cDNA from Soybean	Goto (1999)	Iron rich lettuce
Lettuce	Nitrate Reductase (**nia**)	Curtis (1999)	Reduces nitrate in leaves
Cauliflower	Or gene		Vit – A rich Curd
Cauliflower	Bar, Barnase and barstar		Superior cultivar
Muskmelon	Rabies glycoprotein		Edible vaccine development
Tomato	Rol B		Parthenocarpic fruit
Brinjal	Iaah		Parthenocarpic fruit
Tomatoe (Golden)		2004	Improve Vitamine A

Chapter 8

New Varieties and Hybrids from IARI

- ✰ Hybrid **Pusa Kartik Shankar** and varieties **Pusa Meghna, Pusa Sharad, Pusa Shukti** and **Pusa Paushja** are released and being commercially cultivated.
- ✰ *Red carrot variety* **Pusa Rudhira,** *Black carrot variety* **Pusa Asita** and *heat tolerant variety* **Pusa Vrishti** developed and seed are provided to farmers in bulk quantity.
- ✰ Cytoplasmic male sterility system established for the *first time in tropical carrot and tropical carrot hybrid* **Pusa Vasudha** developed first from any public sector institution.
- ✰ Hybrid DBHL-20 and two varieties **Pusa Shymala** and DBL-02 of brinjal have been released and identified by AICRP (Vegetable crops) and are being grown commercially.
- ✰ Nine varieties and hybrid of cucurbits namely **Pusa Samridhi** and **Pusa Santushti** of bottle gourd**, Pusa Hybrid-2** of bitter gourd**, Pusa Uday** and **Pusa Barkha** of cucumber**, Pusa Nutan** of ridge gourd**, Pusa Sneha** of sponge gourd**, Pusa Ujwal** of ash gourd and **Pusa Shandar** of snap melon have been released and seeds are being provided to farmers.
- ✰ Seven varieties of different vegetables namely **Pusa Mridula, Pusa Jamuni** and **Pusa Gulabi** of radish; **Pusa Sukomal** of cowpea,

Important New Vegetable Varieties and F_1 Hybrids from IARI

Sl.No.	Crop	Varieties/ F_1 Hybrids	Image	Year of Release	State for which Recommended	Key ponts
1	Tomato	Pusa Rohini		2004	NCR	Fruits with thick pericarp, suitable for long distance transportation.
2	Tomato	Pusa Sadabahar		2004	NCR	Determinate, thermoinsensitive, fruit set takes place almost round the year, both hot and cold set.
3	Brinjal	Pusa Shyamla	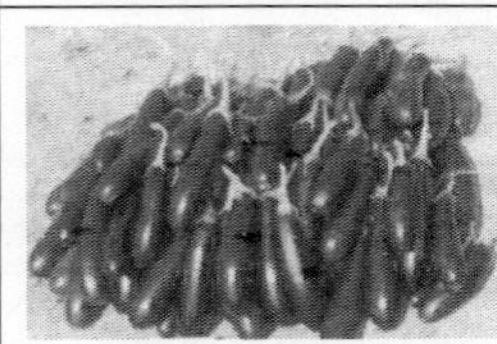	2004	Punjab, Uttarakhand and Bihar	Fruits long, glossy, dark purple, weighing 80-90 g. Av. Yield 390 q/ha.
4	Brinjal	DBL-02	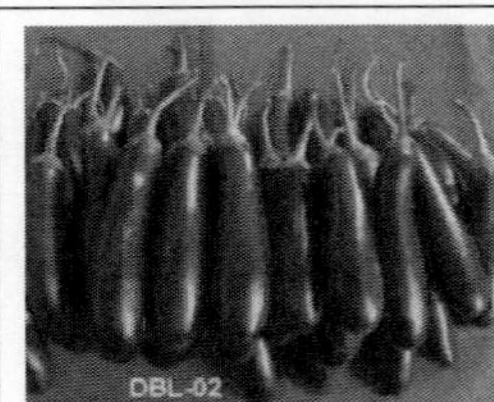	2010	Delhi, Punjab, Haryana	Plants are non-spiny with erect branches, having light purple pigmentation partially on younger leaves, mid-rib and veins. Its fruits are long, violet- purple with round distal end.

Sl.No.	Crop	Varieties/ F_1 Hybrids	Image	Year of Release	State for which Recommended	Key ponts
5	Brinjal	DBHL-20		2011	Punjab, Delhi, Uttar Pradesh and Bihar	Fruits are long, dark purple, glossy, weighing 90-100 gram and it takes about 55 days from transplanting to first harvest.
6	Cauliflower	Pusa Meghna		2004	NCR	**Extra early** (Sept. maturity), white compact medium sized curd (350-400 g). Av. Yield 125 q/ha, maturity 95 days.
7	Cauliflower	Pusa Sharad		2004	NCR	Mid early (Nov.) compact curd weighing 900 g. Av. Yield 240 q/ha, maturity 80 days.
8	Cauliflower	Pusa Kartik Sankar (F1 hybrid)		2002	Sub-humid Sutlej-Ganga alluvial plains and Bengal-Assam basin	Early maturity (Sep.); curd compact, retentive white, medium size, **resistant to downy mildew**; maturity 95 days.

Sl.No.	Crop	Varieties/ F_1 Hybrids	Image	Year of Release	State for which Recommended	Key ponts
9	Cauliflower	Pusa Paushja	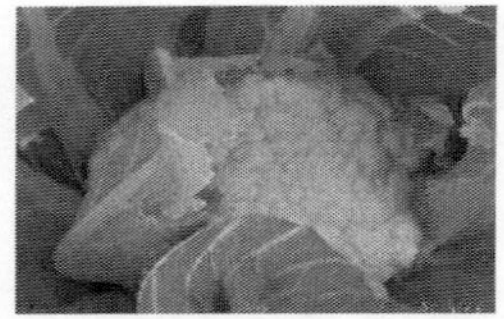	2008	Punjab, U.P., Uttarakhand and Bihar	Dec.-Jan. maturity, curd compact white. Av. Yield 400 q/ha. Maturity 75days.
10	Cauliflower	Pusa Shukti	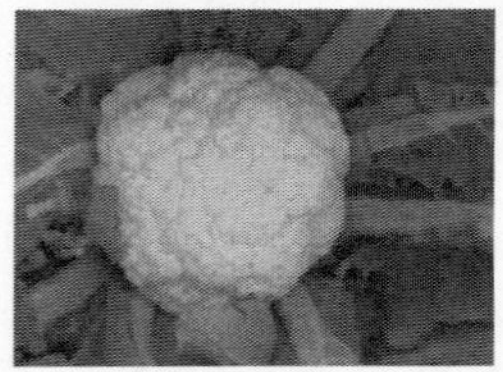	2009	NCR	Dec.-Jan. maturity, curd compact white. Maturity 75days, Av. Yield 440 q/ha.
11	Bottle gourd	Pusa Samridhi		2005	NCR	Fruits long without neck. Av. Yield 272 q/ha in spring- summer and 308 q/ha in *kharif*, **superior in nutritional qualities**, maturity 50-55 days.
12	Bottle gourd	Pusa Santushti		2008	Delhi,PJN, UK, M.P, M.H Bihar.	**Pear-shaped fruits. Sets fruits under low temperature (10-12°C) as well as high temp. (35-40°C).**

Sl.No.	*Crop*	*Varieties/ F_1 Hybrids*	*Image*	*Year of Release*	*State for which Recommended*	*Key ponts*
13	Bitter gourd	Pusa Hybrid-2		2002	PJN, Delhi, HR, RJN, GU, UK, Bihar, Chattisgarh, Orissa, AP	Fruits dark green medium long and medium thick, **suitable for vegetable pickle, dehydration and export**, maturity 52 days
14	Ash gourd	Pusa Ujwal	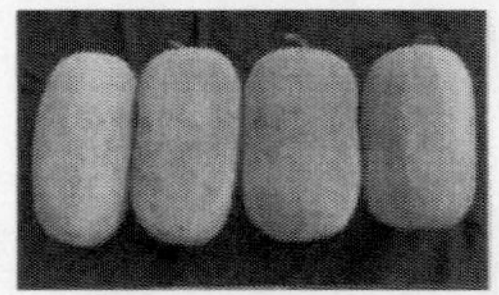	2007	Delhi, Punjab, Haryana	Fruits ellipsoid, **ideal for packing and long distance transportation,** maturity 120 days
15	Sponge gourd	Pusa Sneha		2004	NCR	Fruits dark green, Suitable for cultivation in both spring summer and *kharif* seasons. Maturity 50-55 days
16	Ridge gourd	Pusa Nutan	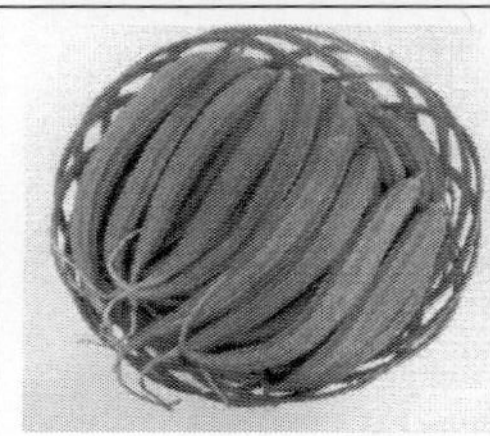	2009	NCR	Fruits long (25-30 cm), straight, attractive green, av. fruit wt, maturity 45-50 days.

Sl.No.	*Crop*	*Varieties/ F_1 Hybrids*	*Image*	*Year of Release*	*State for which Recommended*	*Key ponts*
17	Cucumber	Pusa Uday		2004	NCR	Suitable for cultivation both in spring-summer and rainy seasons, maturity 50-55 days.
18	Cucumber	Pusa Barkha		2012	NCR	First extra early improved variety of cucumber, **field tolerant to high humidity, high temperature and downy mildew disease.**
19	Snap melon	Pusa Shandar	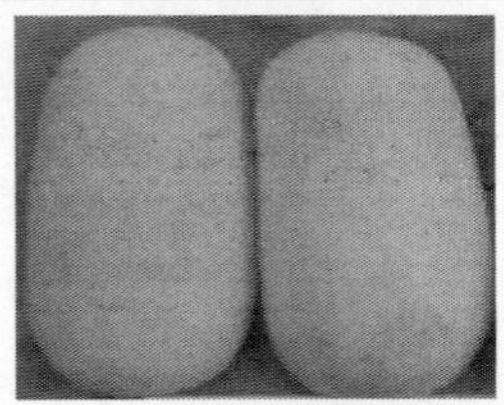	2004	NCR	Fruits oblong, medium in size with **creamy white skin, thick and light pink flesh**, maturity 45-50 days.
20	Radish	Pusa Mridula	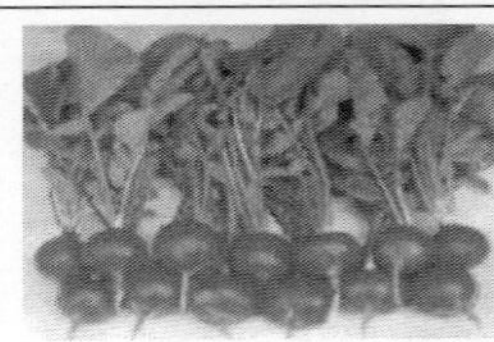	2005	NCR	Roots are **globular with bright red skin, mildly pungent**. Maturity 25 days.

Sl.No.	*Crop*	*Varieties/ F_1 Hybrids*	*Image*	*Year of Release*	*State for which Recommended*	*Key ponts*
21	Radish	Pusa Jamuni	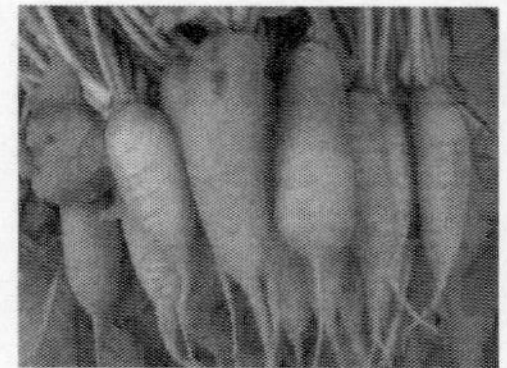	2012	NCR	First purple fleshed unique trait **nutritionally rich radish variety**. Distinct advantage in consumer preference over the existing varieties. **Higher anthocyanins and ascorbic acid.**
22	Radish	Pusa Gulabi		2012	NCR	First entire pink fleshed unique trait nutritional rich radish variety. Consumer preference over the existing varieties. **High total carotenoids, anthocyanins and optimal ascorbic acid.**
23	Carrot	Pusa Rudhira		2008	NCR	Pusa Kesar, besides, being **self core red coloured with delayed bolting**. Maturity 85- 90 days.
24	Carrot	Pusa Asita		2008	NCR	**Self black coloured and late bolter.** Maturity 95-100 days.

Sl.No.	Crop	Varieties/ F_1 Hybrids	Image	Year of Release	State for which Recommended	Key ponts
25	Carrot	Pusa Vrishti		2009	NCR	It is a new **heat tolerant tropical carrot variety.** It is suitable for early sowing beginning in July under North Indian plains. Maturity 85-90 days.
26	Carrot	Pusa Vasuda		2012	NCR	**First public sector tropical carrot hybrid developed using CMS system.** Self red coloured carrot hybrid. High in total carotenoids, lycopene, TSS and minerals.
27	Onion	Sel- 126		2011	Delhi, UP, HR, Bihar and PJ, RJ and Gujarat, MP, Chattishgarh and Orissa)	Bulbs are compact, flat globe, and brownish in colour with high TSS 170 ± 2 0Brix. Single bulb weight ranges from 70.0 – 100.0 g. **Suitable for storage, drying, processing and export.**
28	Onion	Pusa Riddhi		2012	NCR	single bulb weight ranges from 70.0 – 100.0 g., **pungent and rich in antioxidant** (quercetin 107.42 mg/100g). Suitable for kharif and rabi crop, storage, and export.

Sl.No.	Crop	Varieties/ F_1 Hybrids	Image	Year of Release	State for which Recommended	Key ponts
29	Cowpea	Pusa Sukomal		2005	NCR	Resistant to golden yellow mosaic virus and leaf spot diseases. Maturity 55-60 days.
30	Vegetable mustard	Pusa Sag-1		2004	NCR	Leaves large, broad, glabrous, smooth and attractive green, higher in carotene and ascorbic acid. Maturity 35 days
31	Bunching Onion	Pusa Soumya		2012	NCR	**First bunching onion variety proposed for commercial cultivation in India**, suitable for round the year green onion production. The variety is least affected by pests and diseases.
32	Broad Bean	Pusa Udit	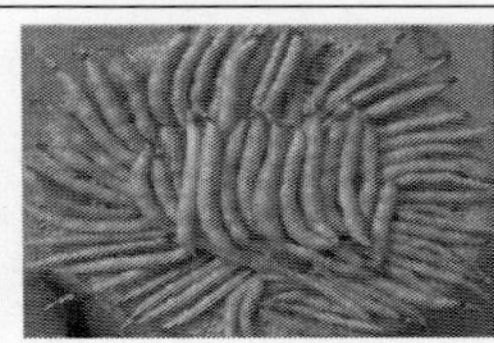	2012	NCR	Pods are extra long, flattish and light green. This is a dual purpose broad bean variety. The variety is suitable for packaging and transport.

Pusa Udit of broad bean, **Pusa Soumya** of bunching onion and **Pusa sag-1** of leafy mustard have been released and identified for commercial cultivation.

- ☆ Two molecular markers **RAPD** and **ISSR** were developed as ***close flanking to black rot resistant gene at 1.6 cM*** distance in cauliflower.
- ☆ Onion variety **Sel-126** and **Pusa Riddhi** (Sel-383) has been identified for commercial cultivation.
- ☆ ***Ogura*** **CMS** system have been established in all the maturity group of cauliflower and is being used in hybrid development.

1) Improved Open Pollinated Varieties from IARI

Crop	*Varieties*
Amaranth	Chhoti Chaulai, Badi Chaulai, Pusa Kirti, Pusa Kiran, Pusa Lal Chaulai
Ash gourd	Pusa Ujwal
Asparagus	Perfection
Beet root	Crimson Globe, Detroit Dark Red
Bitter gourd	Pusa Do Mausami, Pusa Vishesh
Bottle gourd	Pusa Summer Prolific Long, Pusa Summer Prolific Round, Pusa Naveen, Pusa Sandesh
Brinjal	Pusa Purple Long, Pusa Purple Round, Pusa Purple Cluster, Pusa Kranti, Pusa Bhairav, Pusa Upkar, Pusa Uttam, Pusa Bindu, Pusa Anupam, Pusa Ankur
Broccoli	Pusa Broccoli Kt S-1
Brussel sprout	Hilds Ideal
Cabbage	Golden Acre, Pusa Drum Head, Pusa Mukta, Pusa Ageti
Carrot	Nantes, Chantaney, Pusa Kesar, Pusa Meghali, Pusa Yamdagni
Cauliflower	Pusa Katki, Pusa Deepali, D-96, Pusa Sharad, Pusa Shubhra, Pusa Himjyoti, Snowball-16, Pusa Snowball-1, Pusa Snowball-2, Pusa Snowball K-1, Pusa Meghna
Celery	Standard Bearer, Ford Hook Emperor, Wrights Grove Giant
Chenopodium	Pusa Bathua-1
Chilli	NP 46A, Pusa Jwala, Pusa Sadabahar
Cluster bean	Pusa Mausami, Pusa Sadabahar, Pusa Naubahar
Cowpea	Pusa Phalguni, Pusa Barsati, Pusa Dofasli, Pusa Komal
Cucumber	Japanese Long Green, Straight-8, Pusa Uday
Fenugreek	Pusa Early Bunching, Pusa Kasuri
French bean	Pusa Parvati, Kentucky Wonder, Pusa Himlata
Garden pea	Asauji, Early Badger, Little Marvel, Arkel, Meteor, Early Giant, NP 29, Bonneville, Sylvia, Lincoln, Pusa Pragati

Crop	*Varieties*
Knol khol	White Vienna, Purple Vienna
Lablab bean (Sem)	Pusa Early Prolific, Pusa Sem2, Pusa Sem-3
Lettuce	Great Lakes, Chinese Yellow
Muskmelon	Pusa Sharbati, Pusa Madhuras, DMDR2
Mustard	Pusa Sag-1
Okra	Pusa Makhmali, Perkin's Long Green, Sel.2, Sel.6, Pusa Sawani, Pusa A-4
Onion	Pusa Red, Early Grano, Pusa Ratnar, Pusa White Flat, Pusa White Round, Pusa Madhvi, Brown Spanish
Palak	All Green, Pusa Jyoti, Pusa Harit, Pusa Bharati
Paprika	Kt-Pl-19
Parsley	Moss-curled, Hamburg
Pumpkin	Pusa Vishwas, Pusa Vikas
Radish	Pusa Desi, Pusa Reshmi, Pusa Chetki, Pusa Himani, Japanese White, White Icicle, Rapid Red White Tipped
Ridge gourd	Pusa Nasdar
Snap melon	Pusa Shandar
Spinach	Virginia Savoy, Australian
Sponge gourd	Pusa Chikni, Pusa Supriya, Pusa Sneha
Summer squash	Early Yellow Prolific, Australian Green
Sweet pepper	California Wonder, Yolo Wonder
Sweet potato	Pusa Safed, Pusa Lal, Pusa Sunheri
Tomato	Pusa Ruby, Pusa Early Dwarf, Pusa-120, Pusa Gaurav, Best of All, La-Bonita, Improved Lal Meeruti, Marglobe, Sioux, Roma, Italian Red Pear, Pusa Red Plum, Pusa Uphar, Pusa Sheetal, Pusa Sadabahar, Pusa Rohini
Turnip	Purple White Globe, Pusa Sweti, Snow Ball, Golden Ball, Pusa Swarnima, Pusa Chandrima, Pusa Kanchan, Early Milan Red
Watermelon	Sugar Baby, Asahi Yamato, Pusa Bedana, New Hampshire Midget
Winter bean	Pusa Sumeet

2) List of F_1 Hybrids from IARI

Crop	*F1 hybrids*
Brinjal	Pusa Hybrid-5, Pusa Hybrid-6, Pusa Hybrid-9, Pusa Anmol
Bitter gourd	Pusa Hybrid-1, Pusa Hybrid-2
Bottle gourd	Pusa Meghdoot, Pusa Manjari, Pusa Hybrid-3
Cabbage	Pusa Synthetic*

Crop	*F1 hybrids*
Capsicum	Pusa Deepti*
Cauliflower	Pusa Early Synthetic, Pusa Synthetic, Pusa Hybrid2, DCH-541
Cucumber	Pusa Sahyog*
Muskmelon	Pusa Rasraj
Pumpkin	Pusa Hybrid-1
Summer Squash	Pusa Alankar*
Tomato	Pusa Hybrid-1, Pusa Hybrid2, Pusa Hybrid-4, Pusa Hybrid-8, Pusa Divya*

* F1 hybrids developed at IARI Regional Station, Katrain.

3) Varieties and Hybrids Resistant to Biotic Stresses

Crop	*Variety/Hybrid**	*Resistant/Tolerant to*
Brinjal	Pusa Bhairav	Phomopsis Blight
Cabbage	Pusa Drum Head Pusa Mukta	Black Leg Black Rot
Cauliflower	Pusa Shubhra Pusa Snowball K-1	Black Rot and Curd Blight Black Rot
Chilli	Pusa Jwala Pusa Sadabahar	CMV, TMV and Leaf Curl complex
Cowpea	Pusa Komal	Bacterial Blight
Lab lab bean	Pusa Sem2 Pusa Sem-3	Viral diseases, jassid, aphid and fruit borer
Muskmelon	DMDR-1 DMDR2	CGMMV CGMMV
Okra	Pusa Sawani Pusa A-4	YVM virus YVM virus, Shoot and Fruit Borer
Tomato	Pusa-120 Pusa Hybrid2	Root-knot nematode

4) Varieties and Hybrids Resistant to Abiotic Stresses

Crop	*Variety/Hybrid*	*Special Feature*
Cabbage	Pusa Ageti	High temperature tolerant
Carrot	Pusa Meghali	Temperate type, bolting and seed setting under high temperature
Cauliflower	Pusa Himjyoti* Pusa Meghna	Curds develop in May in lower hills Suitable for cultivation under hot and humid weather
Palak	Pusa Harit*	Does not bolt in plains
Radish	Pusa Chetki, Pusa Himani*	High temperature tolerant Low temperature tolerant
Tomato	Pusa Sheetal, Pusa Sadabahar Pusa Hybrid-1	Cold set variety Both hot and cold set Hot set hybrid
Turnip	Pusa Sweti	Tolerates hot and humid conditions

5) Nutritionally Rich Varieties and Hybrids from IARI

Crop	*Varieties/F1 Hybrids*	*Rich in Vitamin/Mineral*
Amaranth	Pusa Kiran Pusa Kirti Pusa Lal Chaulai	Vit. A and C, Iron, Calcium
Bitter gourd	Pusa Hybrid-1	Vit. C, Calcium, Iron
Broad bean	Pusa Sumeet	Protein
Carrot	Pusa Meghali Pusa Yamdagni	Vit. A
Chenopodium	Pusa Bathua-1	Vit. A and C, Iron, Calcium
French bean	Pusa Parvati	Protein
Garden Pea	Arkel	Protein
Lablab bean	Pusa Sem2	Protein
Mustard	Pusa Sag-1	Carotene and Vit.C
Palak	Pusa Jyoti and Pusa Bharati	Vit. A and C, Iron, Calcium
Pumpkin	Pusa Hybrid-1 and Pusa Vikas	Vit. A
Tomato	Pusa Uphar, Pusa Hybrid2 and Pusa Rohini	Vit. C

6) Use of PGR for Manipulate the Sex-Expression in Cucurbit Vegetables

Cucumber	MH and Ethrel	100 to 200 ppm
Bottle gourd	Ethrel	100 ppm
Muskmelon	Ethrel	150-250 ppm
Bitter gourd	MH	150 ppm
	Boron	4 ppm
Watermelon	TIBA	25 ppm
	Boron	3 ppm
	Molybdenum	3 ppm
Pumpkin	Ethrel	100-200ppm
Sponge and Ridge gourd	Ethrel	200 ppm

Note: To be sprayed at 2-leaf and 4-leaf stage of the plant.

7) Standardization of Sowing Time for Successful Cultivation of French Bean in N.I.

Varieties	Pusa Parvati, Contender, Premier and Tweed Wonder
Sowing Time	
(a) Spring Season	Last week of January and First week of February
(b) Autumn Season	First week of October

8) Round the Year Cauliflower Production with IARI Developed Varieties

Maturity Group	*Varieties*	*Time of Sowing*	*Availability Period of Curd*
Early – I	Pusa Early Synthetic	End of May	End of Aug.–Oct.
Early – II	Pusa Katki	June	October–November
	Pusa Deepti		
Mid-Early	Pusa Hybrid-2	July–August	November–December
	Imp. Japenese		
	Pusa Sharad		
Mid-Late	Pusa Synthetic	End of August	December–January
	Pusa Shubhra		
Late	Pusa Snowball I	September–October	January–March
	Pusa Snowball		
	K-I		

Chapter 9

New Varieties and Hybrids from IIHR

1) Amaranthus - Arka Samraksha

It is a high yielding amaranth variety, with high antioxidant activity of 499mg (**AEAC units**) and minimum nitrate content of 27.3 mg and 1.34g of oxalates per 100g fresh weight of leaves. It is a pulling type amaranth variety with green leaves and stem, yields 10.9t/ha in 30-35 days duration.

2) Amaranthus - Arka Suguna

A pure line selection from an exotic collection from Taiwan (IIHR 13560) Light green, succulent stem and broad leaves. First harvest in 25-30 days after sowing and 5-6 cuts in 90 days. Moderately resistant to white rust under field conditions.Yield 25-30 t/ha.

3) Amaranthus - Arka Varna

It is a high yielding amaranth variety, with high antioxidant activity of 417mg (AEAC units), nitrate content of 37.6mg and 1.42g of oxalates per 100g fresh weight of leaves. It is a pulling type amaranth variety with green leaves and pink stem, yields 10.6 t/ha in 30-35 days duration.

4) Palak - Arka Anupama

Developed by pedigree method of selection from F_7 generation of the cross between IIHR-10 x IIHR-8. It is a multi-cut type, late flowering, medium large, dark green, thick and succulent leaves, low in oxalates, yields 40t/ha from 4 cuttings in 75-80 days.

5) Brinjal - Arka Anand

It is a high yielding F1 hybrid with resistance to Bacterial wilt. Suitable for Kharif and Rabi. Avg fruit weight is 50-55 gm. Yields 60-65 t/ha in 140-150 days.

6) Brinjal - Arka Keshav (BWR-21)

Derivative of the cross Dingrass Multiple Purple X Arka Sheel through pedigree method.Tall and branched plants bearing long fruits in clusters. Red purple glossy fruit skin with green calyx. Green leaves with purple leaf base and purple veins when young. Light purple green stem. Fruits tender with slow seed maturity with no bitter principles.Resistant to bacterial wilt. Duration 150 days. Yield 45 t/ha.

7) Brinjal - Arka Navneeth

A F1 hybrid between IIHR 22-1 and Supreme Green angular leaves. Large oval fruits with deep purple shining skin. Calyx green, thick and fleshy. Average fruit weight 450gm. Free from bitter principles with very good cooking qualities. Duration 150-160 days.

8) Brinjal - Arka Neelkanth (BWR-54)

Derivative of the cross Dingrass Multiple Purple X Arka Sheel through pedigree method. Tall and compact plants Bearing small fruits in clusters. Violet blue glossy fruit skin with green purple calyx. Dark green leaves with purple leaf base and purple veins when young. Purple green stem Fruits tender with slow seed maturity with no bitter principles. Resistant to bacterial wilt. Duration 150 days. Yield 43 t/ha.

9) Brinjal - Arka Nidhi (BWR-12)

Derivative of the cross Dingrass Multiple Purple X Arka Sheel through pedigree method. Tall and compact plants Bearing medium long fruits in clusters, Blue black flossy fruit skin with green purple calyx. Dark green leaves with purple leaf base and purple veins, when young. Deep purple green stem. Fruits tender with slow seed maturity with no bitter principles. Resistant to bacterial wilt. Duration 150 days. Yield 48.5 t/ha.

10) Brinjal - Arka Shirish (IIHR 194-1)

Pure line selection from IIHR 194-1, a local collection from Karnataka Tall plants, green leaves with white flowers Fruits green, extra long. solitary bearing habit. Duration 140- 150 days. Yield 39 t/ha

11) Capsicum - Arka Basant

Indeterminate plant habit with yellow green foliage.Thick fleshed, 2-3 lobed conical fruits Average fruit weight 50-80 g Fruits erect, cream coloured, which turn orange red on ripening.Yield potential of 16 t/ha Duration of 150 days

12) Capsicum - Arka Gaurav

Indeterminate plant habit with green foliage. Thick fleshed, 3-4 lobed green blocky fruits. Average fruit weight 130-150 g. Fruits erect which turn orange yellow on ripening. Yield potential of 16 t/ha. Duration of 150 days

13) Capsicum - Arka Mohini

Determinate plant habit with dark green foliage.Thick fleshed, 3-4 lobed dark green blocky fruits. Average fruit weight 180-200 gms Fruits pendent, which turn red on ripening.Yield potential of 20 t/ha Duration of 160 days

14) Cauliflower - Arka Kanti

Selection from a local collection from Hazipur, Bihar. An **Early tropical cauliflower** variety. White, compact curds. Duration 60 days. Yield 22-25 t/ha.

15) Chilli - Arka Harita

High yielding chilli F1 hybrid developed by using MS line. Plants tall (1m) and spreading (90cm.). Fruits medium long (10 cm) with width 1 cm. Fresh yield 31 t/hectare and dry yield 6 t/ha in 150-160 days. Fruits are dark green and turn red.Tolerant to powdery mildew and viruses.

16) Chilli - Arka Lohit

A pure line selection from IHR 324(local collection). Plants tall. Fruits dark green, smooth, straight, turning deep red on maturity (Capsanthin 0.205 per cent) Fruits highly pungent (Capsaicin 0.708 per cent) Suitable for irrigated and rainfed cultivation. Duration 180 days. Yield 25 t/ha. (green Chilli). 3 t/ha. (dry chilli)

17) Chilli - Arka Meghana

High yielding chilli F1 hybrid developed by using MS line. Plants medium tall (81.3 cm) and spreading 69.5 cm. Fruits long (10.6 cm) with width of 1.2 cm. Very early, taking 24 days for 50 per cent flowering. Fresh yield of 33.5 t/ha and dry yield of 5 t/ha in 140-150 days. Fruits are dark green and turn deep red.Tolerant to powdery mildew and viruses.

18) Chilli - Arka Suphal PMR 57

Indeterminate with a plant height of 80-90 cm Dark green Foliage Fruits straight, smooth with pointed tip, 7-9 cm long Fruit colour green changing to deep red Yield: 25t green and 3 t dry chilli/ha Resistant to powdery mildew and field tolerant to viruses.

19) Chilli - Arka Sweta

High yielding chilli F_1 hybrid developed by using MS line. Plants medium tall (95 cm) and spreading (82.5 cm). Fruits long (13.2 cm) with 1.3 cm width. Fresh yield 38.4t/ha and dry yield of 6 t/ha in 140-150 days. Fruits are light green, turns red.

20) Cluster bean - Goma manjari

Resistant to **Powdery mildew, Bacterial blight and Leaf spot**. Cluster bean - Goma manjari Photosensitive

21) Coriander - Arka Isha

High yielding multicut type of coriander. Yields 3.7 t/ha by pulling at 40 days after sowing and 12.17 t/ha by cutting (3 cuts) Leaf essential oil yield is 0.083 per cent with good aroma. Keeping quality at Room Temperature is 3 days and at Low Temperature is 3 weeks without loosing its aroma when stored in polythene bags (100 PE Gauge).

22) Cowpea - Arka Garima

Derivative of the cross T.U.V.762 x V.uniquiculata sub sp.sesquipedalis Developed by back cross and pure line selection. Plants tall, vigerous, bushy, with small vines and photo insensitive. Leaf colour light green.Flower colour purple. Pods light green, long, thick, round, fleshy and string less. Suitable for vegetable purpose. Tolerant to heat, drought and low moisture stress. Duration 90 days. Pod Yield 18 t/ha.

23) Dolichos - Arka Amogh

Plants are medium tall, 50 per cent flowering in 40 days and pods are ready for harvest in 55 days. Pods are similar to Arka Jay and Konkan Bhushan. Yield: 19-20 t/ha.

24) Dolichos - Arka Jay

Developed through back cross and pedigree selection involving the Parents Hebbal Avare x IIHR 93. Plants dwarf, bushy, erect and photo insensitive. Flowers purple. Pods long, light green slightly curved, Without parchment. Vegetable type with excellent cooking qualities. Tolerant to low moisture stress. Duration 75 days. Pod Yield 12 t/ha

25) Dolichos - Arka Sambhram

Plants are medium height, 50 per cent flowering in 40 days and pods are ready for harvest in 55 days. Pods are flat, light green, medium long (13-15 cm), medium width (1.5 cm). Yield: 19-20 t/ha.

26) Dolichos - Arka

Hebbal Avare x IIHR 93.

27) Dolichos - Arka Vijay

Hebbal Avare x IIHR 93

28) French Bean - Arka Komal

A pure line selection from IIHR-60 (Collection from Australia). Plants erect and bushy, Photo insensitive Flat, green straight pods. Seeds light brown, oblong and large. Good transportation and cooking qualities.Seed yield 1500 kg/ha Duration 70 days. Pod Yield 20 t/ha.

29) French Bean - Arka Komal (Sel-9)

A pure line selection from IIHR-60 (Collection from Australia).Plants erect and bushy, Photo insensitive Flat, green straight pods. Seeds light brown, oblong and large. Good transportation and cooking qualities. Drought hardy Seed yield 1500 kg./ha Duration 70 days. Pod Yield 20 t/ha.

30) French Bean - Arka Sharath

It has round, string less, smooth pods suitable for steamed beans. Pods are crisp, fleshy with no parchment and perfectly round on cross section. Plants are bushy and photo insensitive and it is suitable for both kharif and rabi seasons.

31) French bean - Arka Suman

A F9 pedigree selection of the cross Pusa Komal x Arka Garima. Plants erect, bushy, photo insensitive, early with pods above the canopy. Pods medium long, tender, fleshy crisp, without parchment. Good cooking qualities. Resistant to rust Duration 70-75 days. Pod Yield 18 t/ha.

32) French bean - Arka Suvidha

Pedigree selection from the cross Blue Crop x Contender. Resistant to rust plants bushy and photo insensitive. Pods straight, oval, light green, fleshy, stringless and crisp. Duration 70 days. Pod Yield 19 t/ha.

33) French Beans - Arka Anoop

Bushy and photoinsensitive variety Pods are flat, smooth, crispy with less parchment Yield potential of 20t/ha Duration of 70 days Combined resistance to rust and bacterial blight

34) French Beans - Arka Bold

Plants bushy and Photo insensitive. Pods flat string less, fleshy, crisp, extra large (16 cm) and medium long. Resistant to rust.Yield potential of 15 t/ha Duration of 70 days

35) Garden Pea (Pisum sativumL) - Arka Ajit

Developed through back cross and pedigree method of selection involving the parents Bonneville, IIHR 209 and Freezer 656. Pods 8-9 cm long Seeds bold, green and sweet Shelling percent 55 A mid season garden pea Combined resistance to powdery mildew and rust.

36) Indian Bean/Dolichos Bean (Lab lab purpureus L.) - Arka Jay

Developed through back cross and pedigree selection involving the Parents **Hebbal Avare x IIHR 93**. Plants dwarf, bushy, erect and photo insensitive. Flowers purple. Pods long, light green slightly curved, Without parchment. Vegetable type with excellent cooking qualities.Tolerant to low moisture stress.

37) Indian Bean/Dolichos Bean (Lab lab purpureus L.) - Arka Vijay

Developed through back cross and pedigree selection involving the Parents **Hebbal Avare x IIHR 93**. Plants dwarf, bushy, erect and photo insensitive. Leaves dark green, Flowers white. Pods short dark green. Seeds bold. Pods with characteristic aroma, without parchment.

38) Longmelon - Arka Sheetal (Sel-3)

A pure line selection monoecious plant with angular stem, Dark green, shallow lobed leaves.

39) Musk Melon - Arka Jeet

Skin colour dark green at early stage of fruit development which turns into golden orange at full stip stage. Flesh white, medium texture, excellent flavour with high TSS (13- 16 per cent) and **rich in vitamin C (41.6 mg/100 g).**

40) Okra - Arka abhay

An **interspecific hybrid** between *Abelmoschus esculentus* (IIHR 20-31) x *A. manihot* spp. *tetraphyllus* (Res. To YVMV) followed by backcross. Good keeping and cooking qualities. Resistant to yellow vein mosaic virus(YVMV).

41) Okra - Arka Anamika

An **interspecific hybrid** between *Abelmoschus esculentus* (IIHR20-31) x *A. manihot* spp. *tetraphyllus* (Res. To YVMV) followed bybackcross. Purple pigment present on both sides of the petal base. Resistant to Yellow vein mosaic virus.

42) Onion - Arka Akshay (Syn-4)

It is a **tri-parental synthetic variety** with dark Red globe shaped bulbs. Average bulb weight is 115 g. Yield 45 t/ha in 130 days.

43) Onion - Arka Bheem (Syn-6)

It is a **tri-parental synthetic variety** with Red to pinkish red elongated globe shaped bulbs. Average bulb weight is 120 g. Yield 47t/ha in 130 days.

44) Onion - Arka Kalyan(Sel-14)

Developed through vigorous mass selection from IIHR-145 Globe shaped bulbs with medium large size. Deep red coloured outer scales and fleshy succulent internal scales. Pungent with TSS 11-13 per cent. Moderately **resistant to purple blotch** caused by *Alternaria porii* Seed yield 8 quintals/ ha. Suitable for **kharif season.**

45) Onion - Arka Kirthiman

A F1 between MS-65 x Sel. 13-1-1 Medium size bulbs with globe shape and firm texture. Bulbs red in colour with bulb weight 120 -130 g. **Tolerance to purple blotch, basal rot and thrips**. Long storage (4-5 months) Suitable for kharif and rabi seasons.

46) Onion - Arka Lalima

A F1 between MS-48 x Sel. 14-1-1 Medium size bulbs with globe shape and firm texture. Bulbs red in colour with bulb weight 120-130 g. Tolerance to purple blotch, basal rot and thrips. Long storage (4-5 months) **Suitable for kharif and rabi seasons.**

47) Onion - Arka Pitambhar

Developed through pedigree selection. Mild pungent with TSS 11 per cent and total sugar 9.81 per cent. *Tolerance to purple blotch, basal rot diseases and thrips.* Long storage life (3 months). Suitable for export market Suitable for kharif and Rabi seasons.

48) Onion - Arka Sona

Arka Sona has the **yellow bulb colour**, globe shape, big size of bulb diameter 6.5- 7cm, bulb weight 140.0g, low TSS 100 B, bulb yield 45 t/ha, duration 120 days, suitable for growing in Rabi season and suitable for export.

49) Onion - Arka Swadista

It is a **white onion variety** for fermented preservation has uniform white color, bulbs are oval globe in shape, TSS 18-20 per cent, dry matter content 15-18 per cent, edible bulb 98 per cent, weight 35-40g, small in size (3-3.5 cm) suitable for bottle preservation.

50) Onion - Arka Ujjwal

It is a **multiplier onion variety** with uniform bright dark red bulb color, compound bulb with flat shape,bulb size 4-5cm,number of bulblets/bulb 3-5, bulb weight 40-45g, TSS 16-18 per cent, dry matter content 14-16 per cent.

51) Onion - Arka Vishwa

Arka Vishwas has the **bulb colour dark red**, flat globe shape, small size of bulb diameter3- 4cm, bulb weight 40.0g, TSS 160 B, bulb yield 30t/ha, duration 115 days, suitable for growing in Rabi season and **suitable for export.**

52) Paprika - Arka Abhir

A *pure line selection*, fruits light green, wrinkled turning deep red on maturity. Has better colour (color value maximum 1,65,541 c.u) and low pungency(0.05 per cent Capsaicin) **Suitable for oleoresin extraction,** oleroesin yield from fruits without seed 5.78 per cent.

53) Pumpkin - Arka Chandan

A pure line selection from (IIHR-105) Rajasthan. Thick orange flesh, solid cavity. Fruit weight 2-3 kg. Rich in carotene (3331 iu of carotene/100g flesh).

54) Ridge Gourd - Arka Sujath

An advanced pedigree selection of the cross IIHR-54 x IIHR 18 Lush green and tender, medium long (35-45 cm) fruits with prominent ridges and delicate aroma Good transport and cooking qualities.

55) Ridge Gourd - Arka Sumeet

An advanced pedigree selection of the cross IIHR-54 x IIHR 18 Lush green and tender long fruits (50-65 cm) with prominent ridges and delicate aroma. Good transport and cooking qualities.

56) Roundmelon - Arka Tinda

An advanced pedigree selection of the cross between T3(from Rajasthan) and T8 (from Punjab) Angular stem with dark green deeply lobed, hirsutae leaves.

57) Summer cauliflower (Tropical cauliflower) - Arka Kanti

Selection from a local collection from Hazipur, Bihar. An **early tropical cauliflower** variety. White, compact curds. Duration 60 days. Yield 22-25 t/ha.

58) Tomato - Arka Abha (BWR-1)

A pure line selection develops deep red color on ripening. Resistant to bacterial wilt caused by *Rastonia solanacearum.*

59) Tomato - Arka Abhijit

A F_1 hybrid of the cross 15 SBSB x IIHR 1334, Suitable for fresh market Highly resistant to bacterial wilt.

60) Tomato - Arka Ahuti (Sel-11)

A pure line selection. Fruits oblong with 2-3 locules. Thick fleshed fruits have light green shoulder, ripens to dark attractive red, TSS 5.2 per cent Bred for processing- tomato puree.

61) Tomato - Arka Alok (BWR-5)

A pure line selection and esistant to bacterial wilt.

62) Tomato - Arka Ananya

It is a high yielding F1 hybrid with combined **Resistance to ToLCV and BW** Plants semi-determinate with good foliar cover.

63) Tomato - Arka Meghali

A pedigree selection. Suitable for fresh market. **Bred for rainfed cultivation** Suitable for kharif season. Duration 125 days. Yield 18 t/ha

64) Tomato - Arka Rakshak

High yielding F1 hybrid with **triple disease resistance to ToLCV, BW and early blight**. Fruits square round, large (90-100g), Deep red, firm fruits Suitable for fresh market and processing.

65) Tomato - Arka Samrat

High yielding F1 hybrid with triple disease resistance to ToLCV, BW and early blight. Fruits oblate to high round, large (90-110g), Deep red, firm fruits Suitable for fresh market. Yields 80-85 t/ha. in 140 days

66) Tomato - Arka Saurabh

A pure line selection from a Canadian Breeding line V-685 Plants semi-determinate. Round with light green shoulder. Deep red firm fruits with nipple tip. Bred for both fresh market and processing.

67) Tomato - Arka shreshta

A F_1 hybrid, deep red firm fruits. Suitable for both fresh market and processing. High yielding F_1 hybrid with bacterial wilt resistance.

68) Tomato - Arka Vardan

A F1 hybrid, Resistant to nematodes. High yielding F1 hybrid developed for fresh market.

69) Tomato - Arka Vikas (Sel.22)

A pure line selection from an American variety Tip-Top. Plants semi-determinate.

70) Tomato - Arka Vishal

A F1 hybrid between IHR 837 X IHR 932 Plants indeterminate.Fruits large (140 g.) round with green shoulder, tolerant to cracking with thick flesh.

71) Watermelon - Arka Muthu

High yielding variety with unique character of **dwarf vine** of 1.2 mt, vine length, shorter inter nodal length and early maturing type (75-80 days). T.S.S ranging 12 to 14 per cent.

72) Watermelon - Arka Aiswarya

High yielding **F_1 hybrid**. TSS of 13-14 per cent (brix), average fruit weight 7.5kg with 1-2 fruit per vine. Good keeping and transport qualities.

73) Watermelon - Arka Akash

High yielding **F1 hybrid**. Good keeping and transport qualities.

74) Watermelon - Arka Madhura (Earlier Pusa bedana – seedless)

Triploid seedless watermelon variety T.S.S 13-14 per cent.Unique type, sweet, juicy and fully seedless. Longer shelf life and transport quality. Suitable for year round production under protected condition

75) Watermelon - Arka Manik

Seeds small with dark brown specks on the testa. *Triple resistant to powdery mildew, downey mildew and anthracnose.*

76) Watermelon - Arka Rajahans

Densely hirsute stem, light green foliage with shallow lobes. Fruits medium large, round to slightly oval, creamy white skin, netted with shallow vein tracks at full slip stage.

High Yielding Varieites and F1 Hybrids from IIHR, Bangalore

1) Tomato

Arka Vikas

Suitable for fresh market. Medium-large fruits (80-90 g), oblate with light green shoulder. Yield 35-40 t/ha in 140 days.

Arka Saurabh

Suitable for fresh market and processing. Fruits medium-large (70-80 g), round with light green shoulder and nipple tip. Yield 30-35 t/ha in 140 days. Suitable for Rabi season.

Arka Vishal (F_1 Hybrid)

Suitable for Kharif and Rabi seasons. Requires staking (indeterminate). Fruits large (140 g), round with green shoulder, tolerant to cracking with thick flesh. Yield 75 t/ha. in 165 days. Suitable for fresh market.

Disease Resistant Varieties and F_1 Hybrids Arka Abha

Suitable for both Kharif and Rabi. Resistant to bacterial wilt. Yield 43 t/ha in 140 days. Medium-large fruits (75 g), oblate with light green shoulder and stylar end scar. Suitable for fresh market

Arka Alok

Suitable for both Kharif and Rabi Fruits on lower clusters, square round, large (120g) and in later clusters medium large fruits (80 g), oblong with light green shoulder. Yield 46 t/ha in 130 days. Resistant to bacterial wilt. Suitable for fresh market

Arka Shrestra

F1 hybrid. Suitable for Rabi season. Suitable for fresh market and processing. Fruits medium large (70-75 g), round with light green shoulder, firm fruits. Yield 76 t/ha in 140 days. *Resistant to bacterial wilt*

Arka Abhijit

F1 hybrid. Suitable for fresh market. Fruits medium (65-70g), round with green shoulder, deep red, firm. *Resistant to bacterial wilt.*

Arka Ananya

F1 hybrid. Suitable for summer and rainy seasons. Resistance to tomato Leaf Curl Virus (ToLCV) and Bacterial Wilt (BW) were identified for release at national level. Fruits are round, firm (5.0 kg/cm_2), medium-sized (50–65g) with light green shoulder, the yield being 76 tonnes/ha in 140 days.

Recently, a high yielding hybrid with multiple disease resistance (leaf curl virus, bacterial wilt, early blight and root knot nematode) **TLBWEBNR-1** was developed.

Varieties Tolerant to Abiotic Stresses

Arka Vikas

Adapted to both rain-fed and irrigated conditions. Suitable for fresh market Medium large fruits (80-90 g), oblate with light green shoulder.

Yield 35-40 t/ha in 140 days.

Arka Meghali

Suitable for rainy season. Suitable for fresh market. Oblate medium sized fruits (65 g) with light green shoulder Yield 18 t/ha in 125 days

Varieties Suitable for Processing and Export Arka Ahuti

Suitable for Kharif and Rabi seasons. Fruits oblong with very firm thick fleshed with 2 locules with TSS 5.2 per cent in 140 days. Yield 42 t/ha. *Suitable for processing*

Arka Ashish

Suitable for Kharif and Rabi seasons. Suitable for processing Fruits oval with very firm thick fleshed with 2 locules. Excellent fruit colour (lycopene 10 mg/100g) with TSS 4.8 per cent. Suitable for processing. Yield 38 t/ha. in 130 days *Tolerant to powdery mildew and fruit cracking*

2) Chilli

High Yielding Varieites Tolerant to Abiotic Stresses Arka Lohit

Plants tall. Fruits dark green, smooth, straight, turning deep red on maturity (Capsanthin 0.205 per cent) Highly pungent Fruits (Capsaicin 0.708 per cent). Suitable for irrigated and rain-fed cultivation. 180 days duration,. Yield 25 t/ha (Green chilli). 3 t/ha (dry chilli).

Disease Resistant Varieties/F1 Hybrids Arka Sweta

CMS based chilli F1 hybrid developed by using male sterile line. Suitable for irrigated cultivation for both Kharif and Rabi seasons. High yielding with 28-30t/ha fresh yield and 4.5t/ha dry yield. Fruits. Field tolerant to viruses. Suitable for green chilli market with light green and smooth fruits.

Arka Meghana

CMS based chilli F_1 hybrid developed by using male sterile line. Suitable for fresh/dry chilli under irrigated conditions both for Kharif and Rabi seasons. High yielding with 30-35t/ha. Field tolerant to viruses and sucking pests.

Arka Suphal

Suitable for irrigated and rain-fed cultivation. Fruits green, smooth, medium long (6-7 cm x 1cm), pendent, turning deep red on maturity;

resistant to powdery mildew and viruses; yield 25 t/ha. (green chilli) and 3t/ha.

Arka Harita

CMS based chilli F_1 hybrid developed using male sterile line. High yielding with 35-38t/ha fresh yield and 5-5.5t/ha dry yield. Tolerant to powdery mildew and viruses and suitable for dual-purpose market. Turning red on maturity. Highly pungent.

Varieties Suitable for Processing and Export Arka Abhir

A pure line selection from Dyavanur Dubba, (a local variety grown in Kundgol taluk, Dharwad District). Plants tall. Fruits light green, wrinkled, turning deep red on maturity. Better colour (color value maaximum 1,65,541 c.u) and low pungency(0.05 per cent Capsaicin). Suitable for oleoresin extraction, oleroesin yield from fruits without seed 5.78 per cent.

3) Capsicum

High Tielding Varieties and F1 Hybrids

Arka Mohini

Determinate plant habit with dark green foliage. Thick fleshed, 3-4 lobed dark green, blocky fruits.

Arka Gaurav

Indeterminate plant habit with green foliage. Thick-fleshed, 3-4 lobed, green, blocky fruits.

Arka Basant

Indeterminate plant habit with yellow green foliage. Thick fleshed 2-3 lobed conical fruits.

4) Onion

High Yielding Varieites and F1 Hybrids Arka Niketan

Light red bulbs of medium large size (4-6 cm) weighing 100-180 g with pungent flavour, very firm in texture, high T.S.S (12-14 per cent) and high dry matter content. Good storability for 5 months under room temperature.

Arka Pragati

It can be grown **both in 'Rabi' and 'Kharif'** season. An early variety with attractive red colour, globe shaped bulbs of uniform size (4-6 cm) thin neck and high pungency.

Arka Lalima

F1 hybrid. Suitable for Kharif and Rabi seasons. Medium-sized bulbs with globe shape and firm texture.

Arka Kirthiman

F1 hybrid. Suitable for Kharif and Rabi season. Medium size bulbs have globe shape and firm texture.

Disease Resistant Varieties and F1 Hybrids Arka Kalyan

Suitable for Kharif. Bulbs are dark red of medium large size (4-6 cm) weighing 100-190 g. Globe shaped with pungent flavour, bulb yield 35-40 t/ha in140 days. **Tolerant to purple blotch disease**

Varieties Suitable for Processing and Export Arka Bindu

Suitable for export market (Malaysia, Singapore and Indonesia), gives deep pink bulb of small size (2.5-3.5 cm), flattish globe shape, high T.S.S (14-16 per cent) and pungent.

Arka Pitamber

Suitable for Rabi. **Suitable for export** *(European countries).* Bulbs are yellow in colour with medium size, mild pungent.

5) Brinjal

Major emphasis was given to *breeding for resistance to bacterial wilt* and for high yield.

High Yielding Varieties/F1 Hybrids Arka Sheel

A pure line selection from IIHR-192 released for Eastern dry zone of Karnataka. Tall plants with green leaves and purple tinge at the base when young.

Arka Kusumakar

A pure line selection from I-193 released for Eastern dry zone of Karnataka. Spreading plant habit with green stem and green leaves, flowers white, **green small fruits borne in clusters**, with good cooking quality.

Arka Navaneet

First F1 hybrid with high yield. Fruits are large, oval and average fruit weight varies from 400 to 450 grams and free from bitter Principal. First fi hybrid in brinjal in public sector.

Arka Shirish

A pure line selection from IIHR-194-1 released for Eastern dry zone of Karnataka, tall plants, green leaves with white flowers. Fruits green, extra long with solitary bearing habit.

Disease Resistant Varieties/F1 Hybrids Arka Keshav

Fruits are purple long and *bears in clusters* tender and free from bitter principle. Yield 45t/ha in 150 days and resistant to bacterial wilt.

Arka Nidhi

Plants tall and compact with medium long fruits in clusters. Blue-black glossy fruit skin with green purple calyx. Dark **green leaves with purple leaf base and purple veins when young**. Fruits tender with slow seed maturity and *no bitter principles*. Resistant to *bacterial wilt.*

Arka Neelakant

Tall and compact plants bearing small fruits in clusters. Violet blue glossy fruit skin with green purple calyx dark green leaves with purple leaf base, purple veins when young. Purple green stem. *Resistant to Bacterial wilt.*

Arka Anand

*A high yielding F1 hybrid with resistance to bacterial wil*t. Fruit 4-5 fruits/ cluster. It is suitable for growing in both Kharif and Rabi seasons.

6) French Bean

High Yielding Varieites/F_1 Hybrids Arka Komal

It is a bushy, **photo-insensitive** variety (round the year cultivation). Pods are light green, medium long, straight, flat and fleshy. Yield 18 t/ha in 70 days. This variety is cultivated commercially in about 70 per cent of the French bean growing areas throughout the country.

Arka Suvidha

Bushy, **photo-insensitive**, with medium long (15-17cm), stringless, smooth, light green fleshy pods. Disease resistant and high yielding varieties/F1 hybrids

Arka Bold

It is a bushy variety **resistant to rust**, Pods flat (1.5 cm width) medium long (15-17cm), stringless, smooth, light green, fleshy, with crisp texture.

Arka Anoop

A new french bean variety **resistant to rust and bacterial blight**. Plants are bushy and **photo- insensitive**. This variety can be grown during all the three seasons.

8) Okra

Disease Resistant and High Yielding Varieties/F_1 Hybrids Arka Abhay

Fruits lush green, tender and long. Fruits borne in two flushes. Fruits free from spines, having delicate aroma. Good keeping and cooking qualities. Resistant to yellow vein mosaic virus (YVMV).

Arka Anamika

Fruits lush green, tender and long. Fruits borne in two flushes. Fruits free from spines, having 5-6 ridges, delicate aroma. Good keeping and cooking qualities. Resistant to YVMV.

9) Vegetable Cowpea

High Yielding Varieties/F_1 Hybrids Arka Garima

A bushy type. Pods are thick, light green, long, round, **stringless** and highly fleshy.

Arka Suman

A bushy, **photo- insensitive**, erect, early variety (42 days for first picking) with medium long (17-20 cm), thin, smooth, light green, fleshy pods borne above the canopy.

Arka Samrudhi

A bushy, **photo-insensitive**, erect, early variety (42 days for first picking) with long (20-23 cm), medium thick, smooth, light green, round, fleshy pods.

9) Garden Peas

In peas, the main emphasis was to develop a variety with combined résistance to powdery mildew and rust.

Disease Resistant Varieties/F_1 Hybrids Arka Ajit

A mid season variety, **resistant to powdery mildew and rust**. Pods 8-9 cm long.

Arka Sampoorna

A **whole-pod edible**, midseason variety. **Resistant to rust and powdery mildew**. Pods flat, parchment less, medium sweet.

Arka Karthik

A mid season variety, **resistant to powdery mildew and rust**.

10) Carrot

Disease Resistant Varieties with High Nutritive Value Arka Suraj

A high carotene, powdery mildew resistant and nematode tolerant open pollinated variety. Contains high carotene content (12 mg per cent), high root yield (27t/ha); deep orange, self core and smooth surface, root length 15-18cm, and girth 3-4cm.

11) Dolichos (Indian Beans)

High Yielding and Abiotic Stress Tolerant Varieites and F1 Hybrids

Two bushy, varieties with vegetable pod were developed.

Arka Jay

Plants dwarf, bushy, erect and **photo-insensitive**. Flowers purple. Pods vegetable type medium long, light green slightly curved, without parchment. **Tolerant to low moisture stress.**

Arka Vijay

Plants dwarf, bushy, erect and **photo-insensitive**. Flowers white. Pods short dark green. Pods with characteristic aroma, without parchment. Vegetable type. Tolerant to low moisture stress.

12) Amaranth

Disease Resistant Varieties/F_1 Hybrids Arka Arunima

It has broad, succulent and purple leaves and stem. **Resistant to white rust**. Has **low oxalate and nitrate contents.** Has excellent cooking quality and is rich in dry matter content, protein and potassium.

Varieties with High Nutritive Value Arka Suguna

Foliage broad, light green and succulent stem. Moderately resistant to white rust. *Excellent cooking quality and rich in dry matter content, protein, carotenes, Vitamin C, phosphorus and potassium.*

Arka Arunima

It has broad, succulent and purple leaves and stem. **Resistant to white rust.** *Have low oxalate and nitrate contents.*

12) Palak (Spinach Beet)

Disease Resistant Varieties with High Nutritive Value Arka Anupama

A **multicut, late bolting** variety with dark green, thick, medium large, succulent foliage. Moderately resistant to Cercospora. Resistant to Cercospora leaf spot. *Excellent cooking quality and rich in dry matter content, protein, carotenes, Vitamin C, phosphorus and potassium.*

13) Watermelon

High Yielding Varieties/F_1 Hybrids Arka Jyothi

First F1 hybrid having yield potential of 84 t/ha, with high T.S.S: 12 per cent and has already become popular in Western, Northern and Southern States of the country.

Disease Resistant Varieties and F_1 Hybrids Arka Manik

A major breakthrough has been made by developing water melon variety Arka Manik with *resistance to anthracnose, powdery and downy mildews.* Yield 60 t/ha in 90-100 days.

Arka Rajhans

Released for high yield, good quality and *resistance to powdery mildew.* Yield 25 t/ha in 85-90 days.

14) Long Melon

Varieties Tolerant to Abiotic Stresses Arka Sheetal

Tolerant to high temperature. Fruits medium long (length 22cm. and girth 7.8 cm) with light green skin.

15) Muskmelon

Varieties with High Nutritive Value Arka Jeet

Yields 15 t/ha in 90 days. It is **rich in Vit.C** (41.6/100g).

16) Ridge Gourd

High yielding varieites/F_1 hybrids

Arka Sumeet

Fruits lush green, tender and long. Yield 50 t/ha in 110 days.

Disease Resistant Varieties and F1 Hybrids Arka Sujat

Released at National level, *resistant to powdery and downy mildews*. Yield 53 t/ha in 100 days.

B) Directorate of Onion and Garlic

Onion New Varieties

Bhima Raj

The variety Bhima Raj (B-780-5-2-2, IC No. 561257) produces dark red and oval shaped bulbs with single centre and thin neck. The TSS range is from 10.0 to 11.0 per cent. This variety is suitable for kharif and late kharif season. The highest yield potential is 40-45 t/ha.

Bhima Red

Bhima Red (B-780-5-3-1, IC No. 561258) has been developed through bulb to row selection method. Bhima Red is suitable for late kharif. TSS ranges from 10.0 to 11.0 per cent. Average yield in late kharif season range from 48.0-52.0 t/ha.

Bhima Super

Bhima Super (IC No. 561259) has been developed by exercising selection pressure for single centered bigger size bulbs following eight cycles of selection and attaining 95 per cent of single centered bulbs. The variety possesses medium red coloured round bulbs with tapering towards neck. The TSS is from 10-11 per cent.

Bhima Kiran

Bhima Kiran (RO-597) (IC No. 572766) was identified at National level for release during 1 st AINRPOG group meeting at CITH, Srinagar during 2010 for two zones *viz.* Bulb attains immediate light red colour after harvest. Bulbs are oval to round in shape, have very less number of bolters and doubles in rabi (less than 5 per cent), thin neck, TSS 12 per cent, good keeping quality suitable for storage up to 5-6 months

Bhima Shakti

Bhima Shakti (1156) (IC No. 572769) was identified at National level for released during 2 nd AINPROG group meeting at Ooty (TNAU, Coimbatore) during 2011. TSS 11.8 per cent. Small to medium neck thickness, uniform neck fall during rabi and more than 70 per cent neck fall during late kharif. Bulbs have very good storage life up to 5-6 months. Bulbs mature in 130 days after transplanting during late kharif and rabi season. It is tolerant to thrips.

Bhima Shweta

Bhima Shweta (White El. Comp. Selection/NRCWO-2) (IC No. 572761) was identified at National Level for release during IInd AINPOG group meeting at Ooty (TNAU, Coimbatore) during 2011. It is tolerant to thrips.

Bhima Shubra

Bhima Shubra (w-009) (IC No. 572763) released at institute level during 2010 for kharif and late kharif season for Maharashtra region. Average marketable yield during kharif is 24.16 t/ha and during late kharif 38.9 t/ha can fill the gap for processing from October to February.

Garlic Variety

Bhima Omkar

Bhima Omkar (IC 569789), can be successfully grown in the tropical growing areas of India and has been recommended for cultivation in Zone VI. Based on four years screening, the variety was found to be susceptible to thrips.

Bhima Purple

Bhima Purple (IC 570742), can be successfully grown in the tropical growing areas of India and has been recommended for cultivation in Zone III.

C) CPRI, Located Shimla HP

CPRI at Shimla has developed two new potato varieties **Kufri Himsona** for cultivation, in the Himachal Pradesh Hills and **Kufri Sadabahar** for Uttar Pradesh Plains.

Potato New Varieties

Kufri Himsona

It is first potato processing variety released for cultivation in the hills of Himachal Pradesh. This variety contains more than 22 *per cent high dry matter and low sugars i.e.* less than 100mg per 100 g of fresh potato weight. It produces **excellent white chips** on frying.

Kufri Chipsona-1, Kufri Chipsona-2 and Kufri Chipsona-3

Suitable processing varieties for cultivation in the hills so as to maintain the round the year availability of raw material for processing units located in the plains.

Kufri Frysona

Variety resistant to late blight disease. Average one can have 25-30 tonnes of potatoes per hectare with more than *30-35 per cent French fry grade tubers.*

D) Outlines of Vegetable Science

1) Tomato Male Sterility and other Vegetable

Type of Male Sterility	*Inheritance (Gene control)*	*Vegetable Crops*
Stamina sterility/structural	Genic (single recessive) or sl-2	Tomato
Functional male sterility(FMS) 1) Positional sterility or closed anther mutant	Genic (single recessive) or ps-2	Tomato, brinjal and sweet pepper
2) Excerted stigma	Genic (single recessive)	Tomato
Pollen sterility or Sporogenus	Cytoplasmic (CMS)	Carrot, Cucumber, Sweet pepper and Chinese cabbage
	Genic (GMS) 1) Single ressive	Tomato, Brinjal, Pea, Muskmelon, Watermelon, Chilli, Limabean, Cucumber and all cole crops
	Genic (GMS) 2) Duplicate dominant genes	Cauliflower
	CGMS 1) Single recessive 2) Two recessive 3) Single dominant	 Onion, Radish and S.pepper Beetroot Carrot

2) Inherent Mechanism Favouring Cross Pollination

Self-incompatibility	*Male Sterility*	*Dichogamy*	
		Protandry	*Protogyny*
All cole crops, radish, turnip and beet	Tomato, brinjal, chilli, muskmelon, onion, carrot, sweetpotato and cole crop	Onion, carrot, beet, parsley, moringa and leek	EFY, okra, cole crops and chekrumanis

3) Isolation Distance and Field Inspections of Important Vegetables

Crops	*FS (m)*	*CS (m)*	*Crops*	*Number of inspection*
Potato	5	5	Tomato, brinjal, potato, chilli, okrapea, cabbage, chinese cabbage, radish, turnip (root to seed), beet, lettuce and cucurbits	3
Tomato, beans (cowpea, French bean, cluster bean and hyacinth bean), lettuce and fenugreek	50	25	Fenugreek, palak, amaranthus beans	2
Cole crops, palak, beet, radish and turnip	1600	1000	Cauliflower, onion (bulb to seed) and carrot (root to seed)	4
Brinjal	200	100	Onion (seed to seed) and carrot (seed to seed)	3
Chilli, sweetpeper, okra and amaranthus	400	200		
Onion	1000	500		
Carrot	1000	8000		
Pea	20	10		

4) Storage Temperature of some Important Vegetable

Vegetables	*Temperature (°C)*
Brinjal	10-11
Tomato	8-10 (Unripe) and 7.2 (Ripe)
Potato	4-4.4
Asparagus and root crop	0
Onion and garlic	0 and 65-75 per cent rh
Cole crops	0-1.7
Okra	8-9

5) Critical Stage of Irrigation (CSI)

Crop	*Stage of Growth*
Tomato and brinjal	Flower, fruit set and after each harvest
Chilli	10th leaf to flower, to fruiting and after periodical harvests
Potato	Stolon formation, tuberisation and tuber enlargement
Watermelon, muskmelon, pumpkin, cucumber, gourds and ummersquash	Flowerbud development and early fruit development
Cabbage	Head formation and enlargement
Cauliflower	Throughout the whole vegetation period
Broccoli	Early stage of development
Onion	Bulb formation and enlargement
Radish, carrot, beetroot, turnip, elery and leafy vegetables	Constant water supply during the whole vegetation period
Okra	After fruitset
EFY	Shoot emergence
Sweet potato	40-45 days after planting at tuber formation
Pea	Beginning of flower bud development and pod filling
Lettuce	Head formation
Frenchbean and hyacinth bean	Flowering and pod development
Cowpea	Prior to flowering and after pod set

6) Important Disorders in Vegetable

Crops	*Disorder*	*Control*
Tomato	Blossom end rot (BER)	Cacl2 at 0.5 per cent
	Fruit cracking	Borax at 0.3-0.4 per cent
	Puffiness	Reason: Non-fertilization and Embryo abortion after normal fertilization
	Gold fleck	High p,ca and increase mg in fruit
Brinjal	Poor fruitset	Appli 2ppm 2,4-D at flowering
Chilli	BER	Judicious and timely irrigation
	Flower and fruit vdrop	Foliar appli 50ppm at full bloom stage and appli of tricontanol
Cole crop	Whip tail	Soil appli 1.5kg sodium or ammonium molybdate Foliar spray 0.1 per cent ammonium molybdate
	Buttoning	Age of seedling #>5 weeks Adequate supply of nitrogen

7) Important Disease and Resistant Source (Wild Species)

Crop	*Disease*	*Resistant Species*
Potato	Late blight	*S. tuberosum ssp andigena, S. demissum* and *S. stoloniferum*
Tomato	Fusarium wilt	*S. pimpinellifolium* and *S. hirsutum*
	Bacterial wilt	*S. pimpinellifolium* and *S. hirsutum f. glabratum*
	Leaf curl	*S. peruvianum, S. pimpinellifolium* and *S. hirsutum* f. *glabratum*
Brinjal	Bacterial wilt	*S. sisimbrifolium, S. integrifolium*
	Phomopsis blight	*S. xanthocarpum, S. indicum, S. khasianum* and *S. sisimbrifolium*
	Little leaf	*S. viarum and S. incanum*
Chilli	Phytopthora fruit rot	*C. frutescens*
	Leaf curl	*C. frutescens*
	Anthracnose	*C. baccatum* and *C. chinense*
Okra	YVMV	*A.manihot* ssp. *Manihot* and *A. manihot* ssp. *tetraphyllus*
Onion	Purple blotch	*Allium fistulosum*
Cabbage	Club root	*B. napus* and *B. campestris*
Cauliflower	White rust	*B. caribata*

8) Disease Resistant Varieties Developed by State Agriculture University (SAU)

Crops	*Disease*	*Resistant or Tolerant Variety*	*Institute*
Potato	Late blight	Kufri Jyoti, KMmoti, K Khasigaro, K Megha, K Kanchan, K Kuber and K Naveen	CRI, Shimla
Tomato	Bacterial wilt	Arka Alok, Arka Abha, Utkal Pallavi, U Deepti	IIHR Orissa, Bhubaneswar
	Verticillium and fusarium wilt	Pant Bahar	GBPUA&T
	Leaf curl virus	Hissar Anmol and Hissar Gaurav	HAU, Hissar
Brinjal	Bacterial wilt	Arka Keshav, Arka Nidhi, Arka Neelkanth PPC (Pusa Purple Cluster), Pusa Anupamn and Pant Rituraj	IIHR IARI GBPUA&T

Crops	*Disease*	*Resistant or Tolerant Variety*	*Institute*
	Phomopsis blight	Pusa Bhairav	IARI
	Bacterial wilt and phomopsis blight	Pant Samrat	GBPUA&T
Chilli	Leaf curl virus	Pusa Jwala, Pusa Sadabahar and Pant C-1	IARI
	Leaf curl and CMV	Punjab Lal	Ludhiana
	TMV, wilt and die back	Punjab Surkh	PAU
Sweet paper	Bacterial wilt	Arka Gaurav	IIHR
Okra	YVMV	Arka Anamika, Arka Abhay	IIHR
		Punjab-7 and Punjab Padmini	PAU
Pea	Powdery mildew	Arka Ajit (FC-1)	IIHR
French bean	Leaf spot and BCMV	Pant Anupama	GBPUA&T
Cowpea	Bacterial blight	Pusa Komal	IARI
	Golden mosaic virus (GMV)	Bidhan Barbate-1	BCKV
Muskmelon	Powdery mildew	Arka Rajhans	IIHR
	Downy mildew	Punjab Rasila	PAU
Watermelon	Anthracnose, powdery mildew and downy mildew	Arka Manic	IIHR
Onion	Purple blotch	Arka Kalian	IIHR
Cauliflower	Black rot	Pusa Shubhra	IARI
	Curd and inflorescence blight	Pusa Snow Ball K-1	Katrain
Cabbage	Black rot	Pusa Mukta	Katrain
	Black leg	Pusa Drumhead	

9) Following is a Primary Centre of Origin

- ☆ Lettuce-Europe
- ☆ Cucumber-Hindustan centre
- ☆ Chinese cabbage (Chinese Japanese)
- ☆ Bottle gourd (indo Chinese)
- ☆ Yams (indo Chinese)
- ☆ Drumstick (India)
- ☆ Radish (Mediterranean)
- ☆ Okra (Africa)

- ☆ Spinach (Central Asia)
- ☆ Leek (Near east)
- ☆ Sweet potato (Central America)
- ☆ Cassava (South America)

10) Pollination Type of Vegetables

Often cross pollination (OCP) – Okra, Brinja, Chilli, Lima bean, SP-Dolichos bean, CP-sweet potato, Spinach and Palak

11) Type of Inflorescence in

Catkin – Cabbage

Racemose – Peas, Beans, Tomato, Cole Crops (Except Brocolli-Cynae)

Spike – Amaranthus, Palak Panicle – Drumstick and Cassava, Onion, Celery, Garlic, Umbel - Beet

Spadix - Colocassia Head - Lettuce, EFY

Capitullum – Globe artichoch

12) Which of the following is Insect Pollinated

Onion, Radish and Carrot

13) Following Mechanism Favour for Cross Pollination

Brinjal - Heterostyly Cole crop - Protogyny Carrot – Protoandry

14) Edible Part of some of the Vegetables

Corm – yam

Bulb-onion and garlic

Root-horse radish, celeriac, salisfy, Rutabaga, Parsnip and Jerusalam Artichock Leaf-newzealand spinach, leek and Basella

15) Almost all the Vegetable Crops belongs to the Plant Sub Community (Bryophyte)

16) Nutritive Value of Vegetable

- ☆ Oxalic acid – Amaranth, Basella and Portulaca
- ☆ Solasodine – Brinjal
- ☆ Phytic acid, Trypsine inhibitor and anti Vit-E – peas and beans

- ✰ Saponine – Spinach, Tomato and Asparagus
- ✰ Apiin – celery
- ✰ Cheratin – Bitter gourd
- ✰ Malic acid – Carrot, celery and lettuce
- ✰ Citric acid – Potato, beetroot and tomato
- ✰ Selenium – Act as a anti-oxidant

16) Cool Season Vegetable min Soil Temp. for Germination (1.7 to 4.4°C)

17) Warm Season Vegetable min Soil Temp. for Germination (15°C)

18) Tomato Temperature

15°C to 21°C – Critical night tep. for fruit set 21-24°C - Best for lycopene development

<13°C or > 32°C – Fruits fail to set

10-25°C – Ideal temp. for both red and yello colours

>30°C – Red colour suppressed

21°C - Optimum tep. For pollination

>40°C – Lycopene pigment destroyed

19) Important Vegetable Variety and Introduction

Crop	*Variety*	*Country*
Watermelon	Sugar Baby	USA
Tomato	Dwarf Money Maker Roma, Labonita, Sioux, Best of All and Marvel	USA
Cauliflower	Improved Japanese	Israel
Cabbage	Golden Acre	Denmark
Cowpea	Pusa Barsati	Philippines
Lettuce	Great Lakes	USA
Pea	Bonneville, Early Badger, Lincon, Alderman and Perfection New Line	UAS
	Arkel, Early Superb, Meteor, Alaska and Little Marvel	France(UK)
	Sylvia	Sweden

Crop	*Variety*	*Country*
French bean	Arka Komal	Australia
	Contender, Giant Strigless, Ketucky Wonder, Bountiful, Master Piece and Premier	USA
	Jampa	Mexico
Watermelon	Asahi Yamata	Japan
Sweet pepper	California Wonder, Chinese Giant and Bullnose	USA

Hyacinth bean hybrids **Arka jay, Arka vijay and Konkan bhusan** female parentage (**Hebbel Avare**)

Parentage of **Arka Abhay, Arka Anamika**(*A.es.X A.m.ssp tetraphyllus*) and **Punjab-7, Punjab padmini and parbhani kranti** (*A.esculenta x A.manihot ssp manihot*)

21) Mutation Breeding in Vegetable Crops and Varieties

Crops	*Variety*	*Source of Mutation*
Tomato	S-12	X-ray mutant of Sioux
	CO-3 (Marutham)	Mutant of CO-1
	Pusa Lal Meeruti	Gama ray mutant of Meeruti
French bean	Pusa Parbati	X-ray mutant of yellow Wax pod
Chilli	MDU-1	Gama ray mutant of K-1
Okra	EMS-8 (Punjab-8)	EMS treated mutant of Pusa Sawani
Palak	Jobner Green	Spontaneous mutant from Local cultivar

22) Commonly Utilized Mechanism for Developing Commercial Hybrids

Mechanism	*Crops*
Hand emasculation + MP (manual pollination)	Tomato, brinjal, okra and sweet peper
Bagging of staminate and pistillate flowers +MP	Cucurbits (bottle gourd, pumpkin and watermelon
Pinching of staminate flowers + MP/NP	Cucurbits (bitter gourd, bottle gourd, pumpkin and watermelon
Male sterility + MP	
Malw sterility + NP (natural pollination)	Onion, carrot, muskmelon, chilli, cabbage and radish

Mechanism	*Crops*
Seif-incompatability + NP	Cole crops
Gynoecism + NP	Cucumber and muskmelon
PCR and pinching of staminate flowers + NP	Summer squash and wintersquash

23) Utilization of Male Sterility (GMS) in Hybrid Seed Production

Crops	*Commercial Male Sterility*
Tomato	>55 recessive genes reported and ps-2 (positional sterility) commercially exploited
Brinjal	Monogenic recessive functional sterility reported
Chilli	>12 recessive genes reported; MS-12(ms-10/ms-509) commercial in India and ms-3 in Hungary
Cauliflower and cabbage	Both recessive and dominant genes
Brussels sprout	Recessive male sterile mutant reported
Broccoli	6 recessive non-allelic gene; ms linked with bright green hypocotyls
Watermelon	Recessive mutant reported; ms gene linked with delayed green(dg) seedling marker gene
Muskmelon	5 recessive non-allelic; ms-1 commercially utilized in India

24) Nuclear-Cytoplasmic Male Sterility (CGMS) in Vegetable Crops

Cole crops	Cole crop sterile cytoplasm derived from *B. nigra* and *Raphanus sativus* (**Ogura cytoplasm**), problem of seedling at low temp (2°C) and solved by using protoplasm from broccoli into cabbage
Onion	Two type of sterile cytoplasm; S and T; S-cytoplasm most widely exploited commercially
Carrot	Two types 1) petaloid (commercial scal in India) 2) brown anther
Radish	Sterile cytoplasm widely distributed in wild radish; occurrence of **Rf** allele is frequent in Europe and Chinese cultivars and **rf** in Japanese cultivars

Chapter 11

Some Important Match the Followings

1) Disease of vegetable

1. Tomato – Leafcurl
2. Watermelon – Downy mildew
3. Muskmelon – Powdery mildew
4. Pea – Fusarium wilt
5. Leafy vegetable – Leafspot

2) Origin of vegetable

1. Pea – Central Asia
2. Bottle gourd – NE Africa
3. Bitter gourd – Asia
4. Brinjal – India
5. Carrot – Afghanisthan

3) Disease of vegetable crops

1. Pusa bhairave – Phomopsis blight
2. Pusa mukta – Black rot
3. SL-120 – Nematode
4. Pusa mousami – Clusterbean

4) Disorder of vegetable

1. Cracking in tomato – Temperature and moisture fluctuation
2. Tip burn of lettuce – Ca deficiency + high Mg content of soil
3. Black heart of celery – Ca deficiency
4. Hollow skin of C.F – Boron
5. Marsh spot of pea – Manganese

5) Important disease of vegetable

1. Sclerotia rot – Cauloiflower
2. Fusarium wilt – Peas
3. Downy mildew – Cucumber
4. Alternaria blight – Tomato
5. Anthracnose – Chilli

6) Compounds in vegetable

1. Diallyl disulphide – Garlic
2. Momordicin – Bitter gourd
3. Mahidari – Black carrot
4. Methyl amine – Fenugreek
5. Glucosinolate – Cauliflower

7) Growth regulators

1. Malic hydrazide – for checking sprouting in onion
2. Ethephon – Sex modification
3. GA – for breaking seed doemancy
4. NAA – for fruit set
5. Ca, Bo – for increase yield

8) Important pest

1. *Aulcophera foevicollis* – Muskmelon
2. *Dacus cucurbita* – Bitter gourd
3. *Earias vitila* – Okra
4. *Cylas formicarius* – Sweet potato
5. *Leucinodes orbonalis* – Shoot and fruit borer

9) Vegetable crops origin

1. Pea – western Asia
2. Spinach – Europe
3. Cowpea – Central Africa
4. Bitter gourd – Tarai Region of UP and UK
5. Curry leaf and Moringa – India

10) Vegetable crops and chromosome number (cultivated)

1. Okra – 130
2. Ridge gourd -26
3. Cucumber – 12
4. Onion – 14
5. Broad bean and spinach – 16

11) Basic chromosome number of (X =?)

1. Potato – 12 (Auto Tetraploid)
2. Okra – 130 (x=75Allo - polyploidy origin)
3. Sweetpotato – 15 (Allo - hexaploidy)
4. Spinach – 6 (Diploiy)
5. Jerusalam artichock – 17 (Hexaploidy)

12) Heterosis first reported

1. Tomato
2. Cabbage
3. Brinjal
4. Cucumber
5. Chilli

13) Edible part

1. Taro (colocasia) – Corm and cormel
2. leek – Blanched stem and leaves
3. EFY – Corm
4. Yam (Dioscoria) – Corm
5. Asparagus – Spears
6. Cucumber and Watermelon – Placenta

7. Muskmelon, Pumpkin – Pericarp
8. Bottle gourd, Bitter gourd, Luffa Snake gourd and Ashgourd – Endocarp

14) Vegetable family

1. Colocasia – Araceae
2. Sweet corn – Gramineae(poaceae)
3. Asparagus – Liliaceae
4. New Zealand spinach – Aizoaceae
5. Indian spinach – Basellaceae
6. Spinach,Frenchspinach,pigweed,palakandbeet–Chenopodiaceae (wind Family)
7. Water spinach – Convolvulaceae
8. Ceylon spinach – Portulacaceae
8. Water cress – Cruciferae
9. Chinnese potato (Country potato) and Chinese artichoke - Labiatae
10. Rhubarb – Polygonaceae

15. Important Scientific Name

1. Leek – *A. ampeloprasum* var. *porrum*
2. Shallot – *A.ascalonicum*
3. Colocasia (Eddoe type) – *C. esculenta* var. *antiquorum*) (Dasheen type - *C.e* var. *esculenta*)
4. Palak(spinach beet) – *B. vulgaris* var. *bengalensis*
5. Mitha karela – *Cyclanthera pedata*
6. Chinese potato – *Coleus parviflorus*
7. Multiflora bean (Runner bean) – *P.c occineus* – only crosspollination ssp in beans
8. Tree Tomato – *Cyphomandra betacea*
9. Tomatillo – *P. ixocaropa*
10. Current tomato – *S. pimpinellifolium*
11. Dwarf brinjal – *S.m* var. *depressum*
12. long and slender – *S.m.* var. *serpentinum*
13. Round or egg shaped – *S.m.* var. *esculentum*
14. Buffalo gourd – *C. ficifolia*

15. Mango melon – *C. melo* var. *chito* (var.dudain)

16. Chinese cabbage (Pak-choi) – *B. campestris* subsp. *chinesis*

    Pet-sai – *B. chinensis* var. *pekinensis*

    White mustered – *Sinapsis alba*

16. Economic part of vegetables

- ☆ Hypocotyls combined with Taproot – Carrot, Beet, Radish, Turnip and Parsnip
- ☆ Stem tuber – Potato, Yam, Jerusalem Artichoke
- ☆ Root tuber – Sweet potato and Cassava
- ☆ Bulb – Onion, Garlic
- ☆ Corm – EFY, Taro
- ☆ Stem knop – Knolkhol
- ☆ Modified buds – Brussels sprout
- ☆ Arrested inflorescence – Cauliflower

18. Vegetable crops tolerant to acidity

(pH 6-5) *e.g.* Watermelon, Sweet potato, Shallot, Rhubarb, Potato and Fennel

19. Vegetable crops tolerant to soil salinity

e.g. Beet, Kale, Turnip, Palak, Asparagus, Bittergourd and Lettuce

20. Very low water requirement vegetables

e.g. Watermelon, Muskmelon, Pumpkin and Wax gourd

21. Very shallow rooted vegetable (15-30cm)

e.g. Onion, Lettuce and Small Radish

Chapter 12

Model Questions

I) Model Questions – 1 for NET Exam

1. Contribution of vegetable in total horticultura production
2. Tomato sp for Vitamin C
3. Tomato sp for salt tolerance
4. Tomato sp for drought
5. Early variety of potato
6. Indeterminate variety of tomato
7. Leaf curl virus resistant in tomato
8. Which state having maximum productivity of potato?
9. Maximum area in vegetable
10. Oxyfluorin concentration for weed control
11. Copper sensitive plant
12. Example of artificial vegetable
13. Chromosome number of *Brassica napus* is
14. Seed rate and spacing of cucumber
15. Origin of French bean
16. Breeding method used to join large tomato and small fruit early tomato
17. Little leaf resistant ssp

18. Vit C having maximum following which crop
19. Tomato dehiscence
20. Sporadic growth of apical meristem
21. Disease in seed crop of Cauliflower in hills
22. Hua1 and Hua3 variety of **Chilli**
23. Vit A rich tropical Carrot
24. Okra originated sp
25. Cauliflower var by inbred selection
26. Canker in beetroot due to
27. Isolation distance of foundation seed in Cauliflower
28. Isolation distance of certified seed in Amaranthus
29. Browning of root in Chinese Cabbage due to
30. Downy mildew resistant in Onion due to
31. Powdery mildew resistant variety in Pea
32. Unstable sex form of Cucurbit
33. Ribosome found in
34. 5-8 ridge angle and flatted
35. Temperature in early Cauliflower
36. Stable male sterility in Carrot
37. Male sterility transferred in Cauliflower
38. Cucurbits sensitive to
39. Genetic symbol of male sterile and fertile Onion
40. Fi in onion developed by
41. Progenitor of Cucumber
42. Perennial ssp of Cucurbits
43. Cucurbits maleness induced by
44. Barrier system for seed production
45. Chinese cabbage requires isolation from
46. Blotchy ripening in tomato due to
47. Which method used for seed extraction in rape seed
48. Green cultivation of brinjal

49. Bacterial wilt resistant in tomato
50. Cluster bearing cultivar in brinjal
51. per cent acidity in tomato
52. For cabbage seed production plants in hill
53. Diamond back moth is serious pest of
54. Red onion resistant to
55. Basic chromosome number of okra
56. Chromosome number of spinach
57. Role of potassium in plant is
58. Role of Mg in plant
59. Which of the following muskmelon cvs have netted skin
60. For salt ssp in tomato
61. For leaf curl in tomato
62. Rick is breeder of following crops
63. Who developed combining ability
64. Radish variety suitable for cultivation in hills
65. Sowing of Pusa Chetki radish
66. Dominance theory given by
67. CV (critical difference) = ?
68. Following crop is short day
69. Maximum exported vegetable crops
70. Following vegetable crops highest production in world
71. Pusa Early Dwarf is a cultivar of
72. Heterosis in cucurbits developed by
73. The word cucurbits coin by
74. Resistant source of Phomopsis blight
75. Sporophytic self incompatibility reported in
76. The chemical used to induce for male sterility
77. Propagation of Moringa is due to
78. Chicken pox is a cultivar of
79. Seed rate of onion and okra both season

80. Snapmelon of muskmelon resistant to
81. Gold fleck in tomato due to
82. In acid soil deficient element
83. Additive variance is due to – and non additive variance is due to –
84. Black heart in celery is due to
85. Bare midrib deficiency is due to
86. The chemical is used to control for powdery mildew
87. Tetramorphic is present in following crops
88. Dioscorine toxic alkaloid is present in
89. Problem of seed crop of brinjal
90. Optimum plant population/ha potato
91. Chemical name of ethrel
92. Cultivar suitable for processing in cassava
93. Example of Indian originated vegetables
94. Colchicines formula
95. Compound present in onion, radish, potato and brinjal
96. Storage temperature of potato, brinjal, sweet potato and leafy vegetables
97. Globe artichoke belong to the family
98. Itching of EFY is due to
99. High temperature on potato disorder causes due to

II) Model Questions – 2 for NET Exam

1. Saline sensitive crop
2. Acid tolerant crops
3. The crops foe low water requirement
4. *Solanum melongenum* cant be cross with
5. The scientist related to combining ability
6. For control of TMV in tomato
7. Botanical name of sweet poatao weevil and minor vegetables
8. CH-1 and CH-3 chilly parentage
9. Arkel pea introduced from

10. Horticulture and Agroforestry Research Project (HAFRP) is located at
11. Richest source of Vitamin A among Cole crops
12. Seed ball term related to
13. Legume suitable for gum extraction
14. Palak variety developed by *colchiploid* breeding
15. *C sativus* is crossable with
16. *C lundeliana* is a source of resistant for
17. Botanical name of African horned cucumber
18. Glabrous leaf marker related to which crop
19. Recemous inflorescence is present in
20. F test used for in statistics
21. Principle of local control not used in
22. Design used for more than 100 treatments
23. Plastic mulch polythene used in
24. Tuber crops having rich source of
25. TSS of tomato sauce and tomato product
26. Botanical name of sweet gourd and little gourd
27. The protein present in snake gourd
28. Pre-emergence and post-emergence herbicide in vegetable
29. Gene responsible for control shoot and fruit borer in brinjal
30. Who classified systematic of okra and types of muskmelon classification
31. The muskmelon cultivar having good source of vitc
32. Perennial pea
33. Black color seed of capsicum sp
34. Chilly erect fruit are present in
35. Element constituted of chlorophyll
36. Buck eye rot of tomato
37. Temperature for onion, potato and sweet potato curing
38. Expectation of yield in F_2 generation calculation ($F_2 = F_1\text{-}p/n$)

39. Salt tolerant vegetable crops
40. Which type of cucurbitacin found in muskmelon
41. The C_4 sensitive vegetable
42. Degree days in onion was given by
43. Carrot variety requires chilling temperature for seed production
44. Which cucurbit crop need for pinching to produce hybrid seed production
45. Which yam crop need for supporting(lesser, greater and white)
46. Nandpuri *et al* is associated with breeding of (in tomato crop)
47. Example of long day vegetable crops
48. Goitrin is present in
49. Late blight resistant *Solanum* (potato) species
50. Original form of cucurbits __________
51. Primitive sex form of cucurbits __________
52. Which growth habit of tomato have high TSS __________
53. Which vegetable family for wind pollinated __________
54. The cole crop produce seed only in hills __________
55. Agathi edible part __________
56. Processing pea variety __________
57. Best efficient method of cooling in leafy vegetables __________
58. Heterosis achieved in __________
59. 100. R/S(root stock) used in which vegetable crops __________
60. Highest production and productivity of vegetable
61. Flavonoid found in onion
62. Sclerotia stalk rot found in
63. Onion classification is done based on
64. Watermelon seed sterile is due to
65. Recessive brown seed coat colour in onion by
66. Per cent of acidity in tomato ketchup
67. F value TMS/EMS = ?
68. Which nematode wide spread in India

69. Seed produced by breeder
70. Isolation distance of chilli for foundation seed
71. Isolation distance of cole crop for certified seed
72. Nematode most found in tropical area
73. Black rot resistant cabbage variety
74. Great lack is a cultivar of __________
75. Diamond back moth resistant cabbage variety
76. Ca deficiency occurred in
77. Fertility direction one direction
78. In rainy season mulch used
79. Which polythene used for irrigation
80. Indian originated vegetables
81. Potato tuberisation temperature
82. Browning in potato is due to
83. Snowball cauliflower temperature
84. Watermelon sterility is due to
85. In gametophytic which one produce fully fertile progeny
86. Edible part of rhubarb
87. Anovas table given by
88. Lowest seed variability found in vegetables
89. Most respiring vegetables
90. Stable male sterility found in carrot
91. Plant produce flower during winter
92. Buffalo gourd scientific name
93. Netted melon in America called
94. Tendril turn into leaflet
95. Phyllody is a disease of
96. Yellow colour of beet due to
97. Anthracnose is a disease of
98. Colorado potato beetle SN
99. Male fertile line in onion

III) Model Questions – 3 for NET Exam

1. Cavity spot in carrot due to
2. Stamen number in onion
3. Garlic pungency is due to
4. Brinjal produce fertile hybrid crossing with
5. Progenitor of cucumber
6. Netted melon
7. Starch mainly produce from
8. Pea threshold temperature for heat unit
9. Biogass consit of
10. Carotenoid pigment in chilli
11. Modern classification of capsicum consist of (total)
12. Herbicide used for pre-emergence
13. YVMV of okra Arka Anamika derived from
14. GA3 for vernalisation of cole crops
15. Pusa Red Plum of tomato is crossed by
16. Pusa Harit cross by
17. When radish is used as male while crossing with cauliflower the sterile is due to
18. Highest vitamin C found in vegetable
19. Vitamin C source of tomato
20. Scientific name of Jerusalem Artichoke
21. The mineral which is component of chlorophyll
22. Dioscorine found in
23. Perennial spot pea
24. Powdery mildew resistant cucurbits
25. Watermelon having good source of
26. Degree of dominance
27. Cassava belongs to the family
28. Number of characters studied by Mendal
29. Which of the following cabbage variety is late maturity

30. Which of the following is transplanted vegetable
31. Which one of the following is not a Indian origin
32. Which one of the following monoecious perennial
33. Following one is white flower gourd
34. Pusa Mukta is resistant to
35. Variety Sree Latha and Sree Kala is a
36. Chromosome number of carrot
37. PPT and FRA came into enforces
38. High solanine content species of brinjal
39. Scientific name of Meta Karela
40. Highest dioscorene present in
41. Little leaf of brinjal is due to
42. Which one of the following is short day plant
43. The resistant form C. *mortinerii* was transfered from C. *pepo* using C. *moschata* was bridging species
44. Pungency of capsicum is _______
45. Which one the following is highly self pollinated
46. Variety of onion suitable for kharif cultivation
47. Ressive epistasis ratio
48. Which one of the folloing is a mother of all marker
49. Which one of the following one is breeder choice
50. Which one of the following is PCR based marker
51. Which one of the folloing ic Non-PCR based marker
52. Following one is dominant marker
53. Who reported the linkage
54. Bitter principle of bitter gourd
55. Pusa Ujjwal is a variety of
56. Following one is recalcitrant seeds
57. India stands first in total production of(Peas and Okra)
58. Which of the following is the leading export commodity of India (Fresh onion)

59. Which of the following commodity has maximum export value(Cucumber and gherkin
60. Optimum generation for inbred line production in carrot (2-3)
61. Optimum generation for inbred line production in onion (3)
62. Optimum geberation for inbred line production in cabbage (3-4)
63. Inbreeding depression is much more among the following (winter cauliflower)
64. Haploid are produced and maintained by (Ather culture)
65. Distant interspecific hybrids in vegetables are produced by (embryo culture)
66. Somatic hybrids of *Solanum melongena* and *S. sisimbrifolium* was made possible by (protoplas fusion)
67. Which of the following is a not a DNA marker(Isozyme)
68. Salt tolerant lines in vegetable crops can be selected in vitro by
69. Quich and potential method of sekcting the disease/Stress resistant is(Somaclonal v.)
70. Potato resistant to colarado potato beetle developed by introducing a gene(cry3 Aa)
71. Resistant to diamond back moth was developed by introducing which synthetic gene in cabbage and broccoli (Cry Lac)
72. Colour content of tomato controlled by (2gene)
73. Resistant to fussarium wilt in pea is (single gene inheritance)
74. Which of the following is chilli variety is a result of hybridization (G1)
75. Arka Anmol a brinjal variety is the result of a cross between(PPL x Hyderpur)
76. Inheritance of YVMV in Okra is controlled by (2 Complementary gene)
77. Pant Gobi a cauliflower variety is developed by (Synthetic Breeding)
78. Pant Shubra, Cauliflower is developed as a result of (Recurrent Selection)

79. Which of the following radish variety is developed as a mass selection (Arka Nishant)
80. Which one of the turnip variety is not the result of hybridization (Pusa Swati)
81. Tomato variety resistant to root knot nematodes (Hissar Lalit, Arka Vardhan)
82. Resistance to fusarium wilt in pea is (single gene inheritance)
83. Tomato varity resistant to bacterial wilt (Arka Abha, Arka Alok and Arka Shresha)
84. Pant bahar tomato variety resistant to (both vertiallium and fusarrium)
85. Tomato salt tolerant species (*L. peruvianum, L. pennelli* and *L. cheesmani*)
86. Bacterial wilt resistant brinjal varieties(Pant Samrat, Pant Rituraj and Pusa anupam
87. Phomopsis blight resistant brinjal variety (Pant Samrat, PPC and Pusa Bhiarab)
88. Little leaf resistant variety of brinjal (Arka Sheel and Manjari Gota)
89. Leaf curl variety of chilli (Pusa Jawala, Pant C-1 and Pusa Sadhabahar
90. Arka Manik watermwlon is Resistant to (PM, DM and Anthracnose)
91. Poinsette cucumber is resistant to (PM, anthracnose and angular leaf spot)
92. *Allium fistulosum* is Resistant to (Neck rot, Pink rot and Onion smut)
93. Punjab Lal a chilli variety is resistant to (CMV, CMMV and Bacterial wilt)
94. Pusa sadabahar a chilli variety is Resistant to (CMV, TMV and leaf curl)
95. Pant C-1 chilli is resistant to (Bacterial blight, TMC and CMV)
96. MDR chilli variety perennial is resistant to (CMV, TCLV and TMV)
97. Nematode resistant variety of tomato (S12)
98. In-determinate tomato variety (Sioux)
99. In chilli blue anthers present in (*C. chinense*)

IV) Model Questions – 4 for NET Exam

1. Pungency present in onion (Allyl propyl disulphide)
2. *S. melongenum* is cross compatible with (*S.incanum*)
3. Among cole crops highly cross pollinated (Broccoli)
4. SN of Choti and Badi Chouli of amaranthus
5. Which one of the following is multicul varirty of amaranthus
6. Which of the following method is commercially exliopted for hybrid seed production
7. Pusa Sumeet is a variety of
8. SN of the tree onion
9. Hakuran variety derived from(Cabbage and Chinese cabbage)
10. Law of independence assortment refers to
11. Variety Pusa Drum Head is resistant
12. Variety which one of the following is interspecific hybrid
13. Who gave the classification of muskmelon
14. The pungency of radish is due to——
15. French bean which one of the following is resitantce source of powdery mildew
16. Co1 species of amaranthus (*A. dubius*)
17. Choti Chauli species (*A. bilitum*)
18. Shallow rooted vegetables
19. Less water requirement vegetables
20. Monoecious perennial vegetables
21. Cassava belongs to the family
22. Pureline theory given by
23. Botanical name of Methi
24. Reciprocal recurrent selection is given by
25. Dially selection and half dially section breeding formula
26. Anthesis time of methi
27. Flower colour of common Methi and Kasuri Methi
28. Dichogamy present in following crops

29. Cabbage classification is given by
30. Chromosome number of carrot and cauliflower
31. The toxic substances present in brinjal is _______
32. Easy crossable sp of brinjal and chilli
33. Diosgenin rich species of yam
34. Edible part of Brussels sprout broccoli
35. Golden nematode is a problem in (Potato)
36. Example of edible fungus (Mush room)
37. Diosgenin is present in seed of
38. Hollow heart is observed in **large size** tubers in potato
39. GLV have good source of Vit E (Tocopherol) and Vit K (Antihemorrhagic vit)
40. Predict the performance of synthetic before formation formula $F_2 = F_1 - (F_1 - P/n)$
41. Minimum soil temperature for seed germination in vegetable range b/w (2 to 15°C)
42. Long day vegetable (8-10 hrs) *e.g.* Onion, Potato, Cole crops, lettuce, rootcrops, spinach, palck,
43. Short-day vegetable crops *e.g.* Indian bean, Clusterbean, Winged bean and sweet potato
44. Day-neutral crop *e.g.* Tomato, Brinjal, Chilli, Sweetpepper, Cucurbitaceous, cowpea, okra, frenchbean and amaranthus
45. Very low respire vegetable *e.g.* Potato and onion
46. Very high respire vegetables *e.g.* Green onion, Muskmelon, Watermelon, Caulioflower, Okra, Leafy greens, Broccoli, Asparagus and Parsley
47. ZECC (Zero Energy Cool Chamber) working under principle of evaporative cooling – summer outside temp 44°c but inside 28 to 29°C
48. Vegetables mostly Orthodox seed except pointed gourd and chowchow (Recal. seed)
49. Hints for Tag color **y**ellow **w**hite **b**orer [BS (**y**ellow), FS (**w**hite) and CS (**b**lue)]

50. Maximum permitted off-types(per cent) for all vegetables FS- 0.1 per cent and CS-0.2 per cent except for potato (FS- 0.2 per cent and CS-0.5 per cent) and Tomato(FS- 0.1 per cent and CS-0.1 per cent)
51. Physical purity of seed calculated by purity (per cent) = weight of pure seed/total wt.of working sample X 100 and real value of seed(per cent) = purity(per cent) x germination(per cent)/100
52. Each palak fruit contain how many seed (2-3seeds)
53. Which one of species of amaranthus day neutral (*A. hypochondriacus*)

Key for Model Questions

I) Model Questions – 1 Key

1. 61.5 per cent
2. *S .pimpinellifolium*
3. *S. chilensis*
4. *S.penneli*
5. Kufri jawahar, K Ashoka and K laukar
6. Sioux, Arka VikasvPusa Ruby and Arka Saurab
7. H-24
8. WB
9. 0.25 per cent
10. WB
11. Cabbage lettuce onion and tomato
12. Hakuran
13. Amphidiploids (2n = 38)
14. 2.5 to 3.5
15. South America
16. Convergent breeding (Double backcrossing)
17. Brinjal
18. Chilli and cabbage
19. Suture
20. Fuzzyness
21. Sclerotia rot
22. Chilli
23. Pusa meghali
24. *A.tuberculatus* (2n=28)
25. Pusa depali
26. Bo deficiency
28. 1600m and 200m
29. Bo
30. *Allium royallo*
31. Arka Ajith
32. Trimonoecious
33. RNA

34. *C. moschata*
35. 20-27°C
36. Petaloid
37. Ogura type
38. S
39. Nmsms, NMsMs
40. jones
41. *C. lundelliana*
42. *C. foetedense*
43. Long temp and long day
44. cucurbits
45. mustard
46. K
47. acid method
48. A sheel and A kusumkar
49. BWR-5
50. –
51. 0.4 per cent
52. July-aug
53. Cole crops
54. Smudge
55. Okra
56. 12
57. Sugar translocation
58. Chlorophyll
59. Pusa sharbati
60. *S. pelleli*
61. *S. hirsutum fsp glabratum*
62. Tomato
63. Sprague and Tautum
64. White icicl
65. March-Aug
66. Davenport
67. SD x Table value/Degree of freedom
68. Sweet potato, Clusterbean, Winged bean and Indian bean
69. Fresh onion
70. Potato
71. Fenugreek
72. Hays and Jones
73. Bailey
74. *S. Khasianum*
75. Cole crop
76. GA3
77. Limb Cutting
78. Watermelon
79. –
80. –
81. Low K : Ca ratio
82. P
83. Additive Variance
84. Ca
85. Mo
86. Karathane
87. Spinach
88. Dioscorine
89. Phomopsis blight
90. 80,000 – 85,000
91. Breaking Dormancy
92. –
93. –

94. $C_{22}H_{25}O_6N$
95. Isothiocyanite
96. 3-4°C
97. Asteraceae
98. Ca Oxalate Crystal
99. Black heart

II) Model Questions – 2 Key

1. —
2. —
3. —
4. *S. incanum*
5. Sprgue and Tautum (1954)
6. —
7. —
8. Ms-12 x LLS (Hundal and Khura1994
9. UK
10. Ranchi
11. Broccoli
12. Beet (2-6)
13. Clusterbean
14. Pusa Jyothi
15. *C. hardwiki*
16. Powdery mildew
17. *C. metuliferus*
18. Watermelon
19. Turnip
20. F test
21. CRD
22. Augment Design
23. LDPE
24. CHO
25. –
26. –
27. 0.5mg
28. Glyphosphate
29. Cry1A
30. —
31. —
32. *Pisum formosum*
33. *Capsicum pubescence*
34. Pusa sadabahar
35. mg
36. Tomato
37. 35-40
38. –
39. Sugarbeat
40. Cucurbitacin B (Cucum-ber-C)
41. Sugar beet
42. Lancaster *etal*
43. Nantes
44. Bottle gourd
45. white yam
46. S-12
47. Radish
48. Turnip
49. *S. demissum*
50. Harmaphrtodite
51. Hermaphrodite
52. High TSS

53. Chenopodiaceae
54. Cabbage
55. Leaves and Flower
56. Bonneville
57. Hydrocooling
58. Tomato
59. Cucurbits
60. Potato and Cassawa
61. Quercetain
62. Cauliflower
63. Skin Color and Photoperiod
64. Triploid
65. Davis (1966)
66. 0.5 per cent
67. 1 per cent
68. Rootknot
69. Nucleus
70. 400m
71. 1000m
72. Rootknot
73. Pusa mukta
74. Crishead type of lettuce
75. Red rock mammoth
76. High saline soil
77. RBD
78. Perforated
79. HDPE
80. Moringa and Brinjal
81. 18-20°C
82. Low temp. and High RH
83. 10-16°C
84. 3x
85. $S_1S_1 \times S_2S_3$
86. Flesh stem and Leaf stak
87. Fisher
88. Onion (1yr)
89. Potato and Cauliflower
90. Petaloid,
91. Cole crop
92. *C. foetidissima*
93. Cantaloupe
94. Acasia
95. Turnip
96. Beta- xanthophyll
97. Chill
98. Tomato
99. Nmsms

III) Model Questions – 3 Key

1. 6
2. Diallyl di-sulphite
3. *S.insanum*
4. *C. hardwiki*
5. *C. m var reticulus*
6. Cassawa
7. 4.4°C
8. CH_4
9. Capsanthin
10. 5 ssp

11. Glyphosphate

A. tetraphyllus

12. GA_3
13. *S. lucopersicum* X *S. pimpinellifolium*
14. Sugarbeat x local palk
15. Pollen germination
16. Turnip green
17. *S. pimpinellifolium*
18. *Helianthus tuberosus*
19. mg
20. Yam
21. *P. formosum*
22. *C. lundelliana*
23. Iron
24. H1/D x ½
25. Euphorbiaceae
26. 7
27. Pusa drum head
28. Potato
29. Bhendi - moringa - curry leaf – brinjal - clusterbean
30. Chowchow
31. Bottle gourd
32. Blackrot
33. lesser yam
34. 18
35. 2001
36. *S. khasianum*
37. *Cyclanthra pedata*
38. Lesser yam
39. MLO
40. Sweet potato
41. *C. mortinerii* and *C. moschata*
42. Capsanthin
43. Lettuce
44. Agrifound Dark Red
45. 9:3:4
46. SSR
47. SNP
48. RAPD and AFLP
49. RFLP
50. SSR
51. Morgan
52. Glycocide
53. Ashgourd
54. All vegetables except chowchow and pointed gourd
55. Pea and Okra
56. Fresh onion
57. Cucumber and gherkin
58. 2-3
59. 3
60. 3-4
61. Winter cauliflower
62. Anther culture
63. Embryo culture
64. Protoplast fussion

65 to 99 see in question it self

IV) Model Questions – 4 Key

1. —
2. Co3
3. Hand Emasculation and Hand Pollination
4. Broad bean
5. *A.c. var viviparum*
6. Cabbage x Chinese cabbage
7. Mendaline first law (law of purity)
8. Dry rot resistant
9. Punjab Padmini
10. Munger and Robinson
11. Isothiocyanite
12. *P. coccinus*
13. –
14. –
15. Onion
16. Watermelon
17. Chowchow
18. Euphorbiaceae
19. Johnson
20. Comstock
21. –
22. –
23. Opening of flower
24. –
25. Carrot and Onion
26. Mayer
27. 18 and 18
28. Solasodine
29. –
30. –
31. Minicabbage (small curd)
32. Potato
33. Mushroom
34. Fenugreek
35. Large size

36 to 53. See in questions.

References

ICAR websites

NHB websites.